YORK NO1

General Editors: Profess
of Stirling) & Professor $
University of Beirut)

George Bernard Shaw
MAJOR BARBARA

Notes by Margery Morgan
Reader in English, University of Lancaster

LONGMAN
YORK PRESS

YORK PRESS
Immeuble Esseily, Place Riad Solh, Beirut.

LONGMAN GROUP LIMITED
Burnt Mill,
Harlow, Essex

© Librairie du Liban 1982

All rights reserved. No part of this publication may be reproduced, stored in a retrieval system, or transmitted in any form or by any means, electronic, mechanical, photocopying, recording, or otherwise, without the prior permission of the copyright owner.

First published 1982
ISBN 0 582 78178 7
Printed in Hong Kong by
Sing Cheong Printing Co Ltd

Contents

Part 1: Introduction   *page* 5
  Shaw and Ireland   5
  Relationship with mother and father   5
  Early struggles in London   6
  Politics   7
  Ibsenism and feminism   7
  The theatre as Shaw knew it   9
  Play writing: the first phase   10
  Marriage   10
  Towards a National Theatre   10
  The first world war and after   11
  Shaw's beliefs   13
  The plays   14
  A note on the text   15

Part 2: Summaries   17
  A general summary   17
  Detailed summaries   17

Part 3: Commentary   65
  The general nature of the play   65
  Main themes   66
  Other themes   73
  The play of thought   76
  The settings and theatrical styles   81
  Characterisation and the grouping of characters   82
  Stage conditions and style   83

Part 4: Hints for study 84
   Organising your study 84
   Plot and structure 85
   Theme 86
   Characterisation 87
   The style of the play 88
   The Preface and the play 89
   Answering questions on the play 89

Part 5: Suggestions for further reading 91

The author of these notes 94

Part 1

Introduction

Shaw and Ireland

The richness and variety of English literature, especially dramatic literature, owes much to Irish writers. George Bernard Shaw belongs to this company. He was born on 26 July 1856, in Dublin, the city which was to become the capital of the Irish Free State. Ireland still had a largely rural economy and a feudal social organisation: the population was mostly divisible into peasants and landlords, the latter often absentees from their estates, living in Dublin or England. The terrible famines of the 1840s had left a lasting mark: a million Irishmen had died of starvation and the other hardships of extreme poverty, and there had been a mass emigration to America. Right to the end of the nineteenth century and beyond, Ireland had little to offer the hopeful and ambitious. Some stayed, or returned from America, and gradually built a political movement out of romantic patriotism, demanding Home Rule and independence from England. For many others Ireland remained a country to leave, if possible; and Shaw was among these. At the age of twenty he followed his mother and sisters to London and made his home in England for the rest of his life.

One reason for this move was the uneasy social position of the Shaw family in Ireland. The population of Dublin was mainly Roman Catholic in religion and associated Protestantism with the wealthy governing class (traditionally known as the Protestant Ascendancy), on the one hand, and with the more industrial Northern province of Ulster, on the other. Both these groups were pro-English for various reasons. The Shaws were Protestant, the family having long ago gone from Scotland to Ireland; yet they were far from wealthy. Although G. B. Shaw's father was only an unsuccessful corn-dealer, he – and his wife even more – claimed to belong to the gentry, or small land-owner class, and they thought themselves superior to the petty tradespeople and artisans among whom they lived. Their son learnt to see Irish Catholics as ignorant and superstitious as well as poor and coarse-mannered. The path to a belief in equality was not simple and easy for him.

Relationship with mother and father

G. B. Shaw was never called by his first name of George, which he shared with his father. George Carr Shaw not only failed in business, but offended his intensely self-respecting wife by becoming a habitual drinker and being seen drunk in public. In reaction, his son never drank alcohol and added vegetarianism to this asceticism. Bernard Shaw adored his mother and seems to have adopted her rather contemptuous attitude towards his father. Yet it was from his father that he inherited his sense of humour, his scepticism about romance or high ideals or pretentiousness of every kind, and his feeling that nothing, not even religion, was too sacred to be laughed at. He claimed that it was horror at his father's degradation that led him to repress his emotional nature and adopt the detachment needful for the art of comedy. But his mother was an emotionally detached woman, appearing coolly indifferent to her son, who felt himself unloved and neglected in a household where his sisters were given more of Mrs Shaw's attention. (The younger sister died before reaching maturity; the elder, Lucy, took up a stage career as a singer in light opera.) Though she did not teach him or have him taught music, Mrs Shaw's passion for music communicated itself to her son and stayed with him all his life. She was herself a talented amateur singer who performed a good deal in public, and for a time the eccentric teacher who trained her voice and conducted the concerts in which she sang, George John Vandaleur Lee, lived with the family. When he went to London in the hope of advancing himself professionally, Mrs Shaw followed with her daughters, leaving her son and husband behind. After two years of working as a clerk in Dublin, Bernard left his job and followed her.

Early struggles in London

Mrs Shaw made a living by teaching music, while her son was without regular work and dependent on her for ten years. He had had little continuous or systematic education and did not go to a university. During these years he educated himself by reading widely, going to public lectures and joining some of the debating societies then flourishing in London. He developed an ability to speak in public and, as time passed, he made the acquaintance of a number of people who were to be influential in the shaping of his career. He also occupied himself in writing novels, though he did not succeed in getting them published. William Archer, who was a journalist, social reformer, translator and champion of the great Norwegian dramatist, Ibsen, got Shaw his first journalistic appointment, as art critic to *The World* in 1886. This led to six years of music criticism, first for the new mass-circulation newspaper, *The Star* (Shaw wrote under the pseudonym of 'Corno di Bassetto'), then for *The World*. It is now generally recognised that Shaw's knowledge and judgement as well as the liveliness of his writing raised the whole standard of music criticism in England.

Politics

On his own evidence, Shaw had already been converted to Socialism in 1882, when he heard a lecture by Henry George, author of *Progress and Poverty*, and he followed this up by reading a translation of the first volume of Marx's *Capital*. He became a street-corner orator for the Marxist Social Democratic Federation, which brought him into contact with William Morris, the artist and craftsman whose theories became influential across Europe, and with Marx's daughter, Eleanor, among others. But in 1884 he and Sidney Webb, who was to be a lifelong friend, joined the recently formed Fabian Society. Together with Webb's extremely able wife, Beatrice, they were to make this Society a powerhouse of ideas, based on research, which they endeavoured to pass on to the parliamentary parties (Tory and, more particularly, Liberal, before the emergence of the Labour Party). Shaw's experience in a street demonstration in 1887, when the crowds were easily routed by the police, convinced him that Socialism had no chance of success through revolution in England at that time. The way had to be prepared by hard planning, patient teaching and reform by parliamentary means wherever possible.

The Fabians formed a middle-class intelligentsia detached from the trade union movement. They were effective in promoting some of the main advances in social legislation in Britain in the first half of this century and could claim to be the architects of the Welfare State established by the Labour government after the second world war. Though his views underwent modification in detail, Shaw remained loyal to Fabian principles to the end of his life, and his major works of political education, *The Intelligent Woman's Guide to Socialism and Capitalism* (1928) and *Everybody's Political What's What* (1944), were thoroughly Fabian in their nature and tendency. He was involved with the Webbs in founding a famous journal, *The New Statesman*, and in establishing the London School of Economics.

Ibsenism and feminism

In 1890 Shaw was asked to talk about Henrik Ibsen in one of a series of lectures on 'Socialism in Contemporary Literature', arranged by the Fabian Society. He later expanded and published his lecture as *The Quintessence of Ibsenism*. The context in which it was originally given partly accounts for the over-emphasis on social criticism in Ibsen's plays and the neglect of their poetic qualities for which Ibsen scholars from William Archer onwards have blamed Shaw. In particular, he presented Ibsen as an enemy of idealism, intent on destroying illusions and revealing the truth about society. Ibsen's *A Doll's House* had scandalised European audiences by its attack on conventional bourgeois marriage.

His *Ghosts* was reported to be even more shocking, and English intellectuals were eager to have it performed in London. Under the conditions of theatrical censorship then prevailing, there was no chance of public presentation of a play that referred to such taboo subjects (unmentionable in ordinary or polite society) as venereal disease and incest – apart from the fact that Ibsen in questioning the value of the family was challenging the whole basis of Western society. So a club was formed, calling itself the Independent Theatre, and a production of *Ghosts* was arranged for its members in 1891. It caused a storm of protest in the newspapers and divided literary and fashionable society into conservative Ibsen-haters and progressive Ibsenites.

In particular, the growing band of campaigners for Women's Rights saw Ibsen as a champion of their cause. In the later nineteenth century, progressives concentrated on changing the laws to give women more personal freedom, allowing them to hold and manage property, to separate from their husbands on due cause, and to have a voice in the upbringing of their children. They also favoured the trend, among middle-class women, towards higher education and employment outside the home. It was at the beginning of this century, especially with the founding of the Women's Social and Political Union in 1903, that the women's campaign became militant and concentrated on a demand for political power, specifically the right to vote.

As a socialist Shaw certainly supported the emancipation of women, but his private attitude on this issue is not easy to define. One clue to it was his statement that his play *Candida* (1894) was an English version of *A Doll's House*, showing that in England the man, not the woman, was the doll within the marriage relationship. It would be a mistake to connect this view, and the long series of dominating women characters in his plays, exclusively with his personal family experience. It is at least equally a reflection on an ideal of woman widely held in the Victorian period: 'The hand that rocks the cradle rules the world' was a popular summing up of the enormous power that women as mothers, confined to the home, were supposed to exert indirectly as shapers of character and guardians of morality, in the age of imperialist expansion. One of Shaw's best known plays, *Man and Superman* (1903), borrows ideas from the German philosophers Schopenhauer (1788–1860) and Nietzsche (1844–1900) who saw the female Will struggling against the male power of Intellect. Elsewhere he mocks at old-fashioned sentimentalists who want a society divided into the extremes of 'womanly women' and 'manly men'. In fact, he seems to have been working out his ideas about women and their place in society throughout most of his novels and plays, and it is unsafe to generalise about them.

The theatre as Shaw knew it

Shaw had developed the habit of theatre-going in Dublin where, for very little money, he had been able to see a wide variety of entertainment, much of it rather old-fashioned by London standards. He went to operas, performances of Shakespeare, sentimental melodramas (a lower-class version of tragedy, accompanied by background music that worked on the audiences' feelings), comic burlesques, pantomimes and farces. As long as they were well done, he enjoyed even the least intellectual forms of entertainment: the physical, knockabout humours of farce; the performances of clowns in the harlequinades, or pantomimes. When he saw the classic plays of Shakespeare, they were drastically cut, altered and mangled, in a manner usual in the nineteenth century, to show off the talents and personality of star performers who commonly did not even trouble to rehearse with the supporting actors. One such star greatly admired by Shaw was Barry Sullivan, a tragic actor whose style was typical of the period: exaggeratedly passionate, heroic and rhetorical, such a style as was necessary to impress audiences in the large nineteenth-century theatres, where most people were a long way from the stage. When it was transferred to a smaller, more intimate theatre, the absence of subtlety in this style, and its remoteness from the manners and behaviour of everyday life, showed up. So it came to be ridiculed as 'ham' acting.

Indeed, since the eighteenth century, another form of entertainment had flourished which mocked at the heroic style. This was burlesque, which aimed to arouse more or less critical laughter in the spectators. Eighteenth-century burlesque, especially as written by Henry Fielding (1707–54), was sometimes an instrument of political satire, and this had led to the introduction of the system of censorship that continued to operate until after Shaw's death. In fact, there was very little actual censoring of plays on political grounds in all this time. Instead, it was almost universally accepted throughout the nineteenth century that the stage was not a proper medium for serious comment on politics, religion, or sex. The arrival of Ibsen's plays challenged this attitude.

Some of the visits Shaw made to theatres in London during his early years in the city are recorded in passages of his novels. Then, following his time as a music critic, he was appointed to be drama critic for *The Saturday Review*. The three-volume collection of the pieces he wrote for this paper, published under the title of *Our Theatres in the Nineties*, is a most valuable guide to what the London theatre was like in the last decade of the century. Certainly his experience of it sickened him of the most fashionable sort of play: the 'well-made play', translated or imitated from French originals, combining shallow feeling and superficial cleverness, treating rather sensational subjects in a mechanical and basically conventional manner.

Play writing: the first phase

The first of Shaw's plays to be performed, *Widowers' Houses* (1892), was written (on the basis of an earlier, abandoned attempt) in response to the need of the Independent Theatre for suitable material to present after *Ghosts*. In this and *Mrs Warren's Profession*, written soon afterwards, Shaw dealt with serious topics of a kind discussed by the Fabians, and employed a dramatic form and general style owing much to Ibsen's social plays. It was soon evident that he would have even more difficulty getting these publicly performed than he had had in trying to get his novels published. So he altered his style and wrote further plays along the lines of burlesque (as in *Arms and The Man*) or romantic melodrama (as in *The Devil's Disciple*), but twisting the conventions so as to express his serious and unconventional themes. Theatrical managements remained uninterested or hostile, so Shaw collected the dramatic works he had written and published them under the titles, *Plays Pleasant and Unpleasant* and *Three Plays for Puritans*. For this purpose he added to the text lengthy and often amusing descriptions of settings and characters, thus making the plays easier and more attractive to readers. This time the device succeeded, and the texts were enjoyed in the study before they received a fair trial on stage.

Marriage

Shaw had found time in his busy life for a long series of flirtations with interesting and able women, including the actress, Florence Farr, and Annie Besant, the social reformer who was to become the leader of the Theosophical Movement and, ultimately, a President of the Indian National Congress. He conducted a particularly charming flirtation entirely by letter with the most celebrated English actress of the age, Ellen Terry. Then in 1898 he married a wealthy upper-class Irishwoman and fellow Fabian Socialist, Charlotte Payne Townshend. It was a celibate marriage for companionship and it turned out very happily. Henceforth Shaw's domestic existence provided a stable, peaceful and orderly background to his career as a writer. He no longer needed to work as a journalist and, in addition to having his plays printed, he was able to lay out money for theatrical presentation of them to a general public. (But he engaged in a further, most famous flirtation with Mrs Patrick Campbell before she played Eliza in *Pygmalion*.)

Towards a National Theatre

From the time of his association with the Independent Theatre group, Shaw had remained in touch with the pioneers who wanted to break the stranglehold of commerce on the British theatre. Nearly all the fashionable theatres in the West End of London were controlled by men who looked on them as money-making businesses and had very little interest in drama. The result of this was that low standards of acting and production were common, and plays were chosen on the basis of what had drawn large audiences in the past; and audiences used to nothing better had become poor judges of quality. The remedy was seen to lie in getting, first, wealthy individuals and, ultimately, the Government to subsidise theatrical enterprises that aimed at artistic excellence. In 1894 Florence Farr put on Shaw's *Arms and the Man* in a short season at the Avenue Theatre, London, financed by Miss Annie Horniman who later endowed an Irish National Theatre. The Stage Society, the most important of the play-producing societies, working for the cause of a new, better quality drama, was founded in 1899 and gave a few private performances of several Shaw plays. At about this time Shaw's friend, William Archer, was working with a young actor, Granville Barker, towards the publication of *A Scheme and Estimates for a National Theatre* and, in 1904, Granville Barker took the Court Theatre to give a demonstration of what such a theatre could offer. The greater part of the money for this undertaking came from Charlotte and Bernard Shaw and some from the Greek scholar Gilbert Murray. The experiment was a triumphant success. Barker trained a fine company of actors and directed them with great skill. Shaw himself came in to help in directing his own plays, eleven of which were presented at the Court Theatre within the next three years. At the end of this time he was generally recognised as the leading dramatist of his day and the most considerable British dramatist since the eighteenth century. *Major Barbara* was the first play Shaw wrote specifically for this Court Theatre programme. It was performed in 1906. Murray contributed translations of Greek tragedies to the repertory of Barker's company and also inspired, and advised Shaw on, *Major Barbara*.

The battle for an English national theatre was not won until the end of the second world war, when the setting up of the Arts Council ensured subsidies from public funds to theatre companies all over the country which were concerned with quality and originality in their productions. Shaw continued to advocate a national theatre until the end of his life, but the fate of his own plays was no longer so dependent on the breaking of the commercial monopoly. It had been established that Shaw's drama was entertaining and that audiences were eager to see it.

The first world war and after

The conditions of the war which broke out in August 1914 seemed to undo all the efforts of the theatre reformers. Most of the younger men volunteered for the Army, or were conscripted into it. Granville Barker was one who never went back to his old profession. All that anyone now seemed to want of the theatre was the provision of bright and cheerful entertainment for soldiers home on leave; nothing which made people think, or even raised perplexing questions, had any chance of presentation in London's West End. Shaw himself was considerably over the age for joining the Army; but the general war hysteria, the destructive futility of the entire conflict, and particular stupidities of its conduct by politicians and military commanders, outraged his clear-sighted, rational approach to life. (Perhaps his Irish origins helped to keep him detached, too.) He published his criticisms as an 80-page supplement to *The New Statesman* under the title of 'Common Sense about the War' (1914). As a result, he was regarded as a sort of traitor by many people who had not read what he actually wrote. The play that he was planning in 1914 when the war began, *Heartbreak House*, was not produced until 1920, and the work he went on to, *Back to Methuselah*, is evidence of how his expectation of stage production receded. For, as he wrote, this work turned increasingly into a series of lengthy philosophical discussions in dialogue, paying slight attention to the practicalities of actual performance.

Shaw won his public back with *Saint Joan* in 1924. By this time he was in alliance with (Sir) Barry Jackson, a wealthy theatre enthusiast who established and financed a theatre in Birmingham along the lines laid down previously by Granville Barker. For the rest of his life, Shaw could count on Barry Jackson to give a showing of the new plays he wrote; and in 1929 Jackson set up an annual festival at Malvern, a country town in the West Midlands, devoted to the presentation of plays by Shaw and the music of Sir Edward Elgar. (After some years when the only Shaw festival in the world was held in Canada, at Niagara-on-the-Lake, the Malvern Festival was revived in 1977.) From 1912 onwards, Shaw generally arranged for the very first performance of each of his new plays to be given outside England. This helped to spread his fame and ensured that, when each work was seen in England, foreign critics had already established its reputation. For he continued to believe that English critics were biased against him.

He visited Moscow and had an audience with Stalin in 1931. In view of his own political commitment, it was natural that he should be sympathetic towards the problems of the USSR and ready to recognise its achievements. He was always tempted to take the opposite side to majority opinion on any matter, and there was a great deal of antagonism towards Russia in the England of that time. He championed Mussolini and even defended Hitler as examples of efficiency which the lazy and blundering English might profitably study. So he brought upon himself the charge of admiring dictators, hardly dispersed by his caricatures of them in one of his last considerable plays, *Geneva* (1938).

Charlotte Shaw died in 1943, to her husband's great grief. He lived on in the house at Ayot St Lawrence where they had received many visitors from all over the world. (Among these had been T. E. Lawrence (1888–1935), 'Lawrence of Arabia', whose admiration for the older man led to his using the name, Shaw, when he wanted to conceal his identity, during his service in the Royal Air Force.) Bernard Shaw continued writing almost until his death at the age of ninety-four, in 1950.

On principle, he had always refused public honours: titles, honorary degrees and even the highly exclusive Order of Merit. However, he did accept the Nobel Prize for Literature in 1926, giving his prize money for the publication of translations of Swedish drama into English. His own work has been translated into very many languages. A number of his plays have been turned into films, and Shaw himself co-operated in the filming of some, including *Major Barbara*. The fortune he had amassed was swelled after his death by royalties from the musical show and film, *My Fair Lady*, based on his play *Pygmalion*. He had wished to leave his money for the establishment of a new alphabet, but realised that there might be little support for this. In fact, the other beneficiaries he named in his will have profited most: three public institutions, the British Museum, the Royal Academy of Dramatic Art, and the National Gallery of Ireland.

Shaw's beliefs

Before leaving Ireland, Bernard Shaw had already rejected Protestant Christianity for Free Thought. His mocking disbelief in supernatural forces led him to accept Naturalism, a favourite philosophy among literary men of the late nineteenth century in Europe and America. He expressed his point of view in the Preface to his collection of *Plays Pleasant* (1898):

> To me the tragedy and comedy of life lie in the consequences ... of our persistent attempts to found our institutions on the ideals suggested to our imaginations by our half-satisfied passions, instead of on a genuinely scientific natural history.

Despite his enthusiasm for the scientific attitude, Shaw was unhappy about accepting the fatalism that might be inferred from Darwin's account of the evolution of species through natural selection; and, as a socialist, he was especially unhappy with the development of Social Darwinism, which fastened on the notion of the survival of the fittest to justify unbridled free competition and the worst excesses of capitalism. He found a way out through the doctrine of creative evolution as developed by Samuel Butler. This emphasised the importance of a non-individual will, such as appears in the philosophies of Schopenhauer and

Nietzsche, in bringing about biological adaptation and development. *Back to Methuselah* with its attendant Preface (1921) presents Shaw's fullest statement of this idea. In his plays, he usually associates this intuitive, non-conscious will with women characters, for example: Ann Whitefield in *Man and Superman*, the heroine of *Major Barbara*, and Joan of Arc – whom he describes as possessing 'vital genius', a term related to the concept of *élan vital* developed by the philosopher Henri Bergson (1859–1941), the spirit of life itself. *The Adventures of the Black Girl in Her Search for God*, which Shaw wrote while travelling in Africa in 1932, shows all religions, all human ideas about the nature of God, as gropings after truth which reflect the degree of ignorance and savagery to be found in the believers. God, he suggests, is the end towards which human life may move, as it is attracted towards something greater than itself. Though he described himself, in his later life, as a deeply religious man, the articles of Shaw's faith are expressions of the values he held rather than abstract dogmas. After the first world war he found it harder to be optimistic about the future, but he continued to insist that mankind must accept self-responsibility.

The plays

All Shaw's plays are comedies, employing laughter as their medium for critical attacks on various kinds of error or foolishness. They all provoke thought as well as offering pleasurable entertainment. But they are certainly not all written to one formula: some are tightly constructed, while others are sprawling and unpredictable; the settings are sometimes contemporary, sometimes historical, sometimes fantastic; and Shaw's character-drawing varies from realistic to allegorical. The extent and nature of the laughter they arouse are equally variable. Shaw was widely read, and a great many influences from his reading were assimilated into his work, alongside the influence of the forms of theatrical entertainment he enjoyed in his youth. He claimed descent from the great classic authors of comedy, notably the Greek dramatist Aristophanes (*c.*450–375BC) and France's greatest dramatist, Molière (1622–73), and from the Elizabethan dramatist, Ben Jonson; he also confessed a large debt to the nineteenth-century novelist, Charles Dickens. Among younger dramatists, Granville Barker successfully imitated some of Shaw's techniques in his own very different plays; but Shaw's truest follower was the leading German playwright of this century, Bertolt Brecht (1898–1956), especially in his later plays.

A note on the text

Major Barbara was written between 22 March and 8 September 1905. It was first performed on 28 November of the same year, at the Court Theatre, and first appeared in print in the same volume as two other plays, *John Bull's Other Island* and *How He Lied to Her Husband*, in 1907. Shaw's manuscript differs in numerous and important ways from the text of the first edition. It has been published in Bernard Shaw, *Early Texts: Play Manuscripts in Facsimile*, under the general editorship of Dan H. Laurence, Garland Publishing, New York, 1981, 9 volumes; Bernard F. Dukore is editor of the *Major Barbara* volume.

Shaw revised the text again for inclusion in the limited *Collected Edition* (1930–32) and *Standard Edition* (1931–7) of his plays, both published by Constable, London, and the one-volume *Complete Plays*, first published by Odhams Press, London, in 1931, and ultimately reissued, in its final enlarged form, by Paul Hamlyn, London, 1965. It is this revised text, with related documents, that is included in volume three of the present standard edition, *The Bodley Head Bernard Shaw: Collected Plays with their Prefaces*, edited by Dan H. Laurence, Max Reinhardt, London, 1972. This text is also available in paperback in editions published by Penguin Books, Harmondsworth, 1960, and Longman, London, 1964.

The playwright adapted his text and wrote additional material for a film of *Major Barbara* directed by Gabriel Pascal in 1940. This screen version was the first issued in paperback form by Penguin Books, Harmondsworth, in 1945–6 and it only gave way to the stage version in 1960. It is included in *Collected Screenplays of Bernard Shaw*, edited by Bernard F. Dukore, Athens, Ga. and London, 1980.

The Preface was written in June 1906 for the first edition of 1907, and a short postscript was added when this was reprinted in 1933; it is given in the Bodley Head Shaw. A new Preface accompanied the printed form of the screen version.

Shaw's typography

Shaw dealt directly with the printer of his plays and insisted upon faithful reproduction of his own preferences in matters of punctuation and spelling. In particular, he objected to the ugly appearance of apostrophes in words like 'don't', 'haven't', 'I've', which might occur frequently in any passage of dialogue that attempted to reproduce colloquial speech. So, where there is no possibility of misunderstanding, such words appear without the apostrophe as 'dont', 'havent', 'Ive', and so on. Examples of his personal spelling system are: the use of an older *e* instead of *o* in 'shew'; a preference for the American-style *-or*, rather than *-our*, in such words as 'honor', and a more extensive use of *-z-*, rather than -s-, than was usual in English texts of his day (for example in 'apologize'). When he intended any word to be spoken with special emphasis, he followed the continental European system of letter spacing (for example 'y o u') and italicised only single-letter words such as '*I*'. The authorised editions of Shaw's plays have followed these practices, except that some later reprints of the Standard Edition use larger type instead of letter spacing for emphasis.

The stage directions

It was Shaw's regular practice to leave blanks in his notebooks when writing the dialogue of his plays and to go back and fill these with descriptions of settings and characters before sending the text to the printer. All this material was printed in italic type, and it has become customary to refer to all the italicised passages in a Shaw play as 'stage directions'. The term is strictly applicable to a fairly small proportion of the whole. The rest was intended to make the play more easily readable by people used to reading novels but not dramatic texts. Of course much or all of what Shaw supplied verbally in printed directions would be seen, or otherwise conveyed, in a stage performance.

You should look at your own copy of *Major Barbara* and see whether it gives the original stage text, or the film script, and you should also look at the dialogue for examples of some of the following colloquial contractions: 'don't', 'haven't', 'weren't', 'what's', 'that's', 'let's'. Does your text keep to Shaw's peculiar system of typography?

The Preface

The Preface was written after the play was finished, and it assumes that the reader has some knowledge of the play. So read through the play first, at least once, and then read the Preface. The summary of the Preface and the notes on it have been placed here at the end of the notes on the three acts of the play (pp. 48–64). Where annotation is needed in both Preface and play, the appropriate note is given in the notes on the play, and a reference back to it will be found in the notes on the Preface.

Part 2

Summaries
of MAJOR BARBARA

A general summary

Major Barbara is a play about the forces that govern society. The plot is concerned with the testing of Barbara, a high-spirited idealist, by her father, Andrew Undershaft, a fabulously wealthy and influential manufacturer of armaments. Barbara's mother, Lady Britomart, belongs to a great aristocratic family, relatively impoverished, and hopes to induce her estranged husband to provide generously for the future of their three children, all now grown-up. Barbara has reacted against her background by joining the Salvation Army to serve God and the poor. She has an ally in her fiancé, Adolphus Cusins, a young Professor of Greek. When he comes to meet his family again, Andrew Undershaft accepts his daughter's challenge to a spiritual combat: to see which of them can convert the other. The first trial is made on Barbara's own ground, at a Salvation Army shelter in a poor district of London. Here Andrew comes and watches Barbara at work, especially in her efforts to convert a violent intruder, Bill Walker. Undershaft gives a cheque for five thousand pounds to help keep open this shelter and others like it, and thus he destroys Barbara's faith in the Salvation Army by showing her how dependent it is on the support of what she considers the evil forces in society. She keeps to the terms of the original bargain and pays a return visit next day with the rest of the family to see the Undershaft and Lazarus munitions factory and the model town for its workers. They are all greatly impressed, and Cusins puts himself forward as a candidate for the inheritance of this business empire, which Undershaft does not wish to leave to his son, Stephen. Andrew agrees to take Cusins into the firm at once to test him. When Barbara acquiesces in Cusins's decision and says that she still wants to marry him, it is clear that her father has won her over. Barbara and Cusins re-assert their purpose of changing society, but they accept that they can only do so by working within the established system.

Detailed summaries

Act I

The first Act is set in the fashionable town house where Lady Britomart Undershaft lives with her son and two daughters, and its substance is a family reunion. The first scene (not formally marked in the text) is an indirect exposition of the situation: under the pretence of asking advice, Lady Britomart reveals to Stephen the family's financial position, their past dependence on her ex-husband, their need of greater financial help in the future, and the tradition which forbids Undershaft to leave his business and fortune to his own children. Finally she announces that he is about to arrive to meet his family for the first time in many years. She requests Sarah and Barbara and the young men they are engaged to, Charles Lomax (Cholly) and Adolphus Cusins (Dolly), to come to the library. Their entrance marks the beginning of the main scene. (Barbara is distinguished from the others by the uniform she wears.) Their excitement reaches a climax with the guest's arrival. It is followed by general embarrassment. Cholly fetches his concertina and prepares to entertain the company, but meanwhile Undershaft has become interested in Barbara's membership of the Salvation Army. He rejects conventional moral views of the wickedness of making armaments. Instead, he speaks of his business as if it was an alternative to the Salvation Army, with its own different but comparable religion and morality. Barbara and her father make their bargain: to visit each other's place of work and take a chance of being converted to the other's view. Lady Britomart's reaction to this conversation about religion is to try and give it a conventional form by calling the servants in for Family Prayers. The others choose instead to let Barbara conduct a service in the drawing-room. The humourless, disapproving Stephen is left on his own.

NOTES AND GLOSSARY:

Lady Britomart: The unusual first name of ancient Greek origin is best known as the name of an allegorical warrior maiden in the epic poem, *The Faerie Queene*, by Edmund Spenser (?1552–99). Shaw's choice of it aids him in his creation of a character that is not wholly realistic, but shows something of the quality of an allegorical or even mythical figure. The first part of the name suggests a connection with 'British'; the second could be a multiple pun: on Mars, the Roman god of war, and the derivative 'martial'; on 'martinet' (a strict disciplinarian); and on 'mart', meaning 'a trading centre'

Wilton Crescent: an actual address in a fashionable area of London

her interlocutors: those who hold conversation with her. Shaw employs a large vocabulary which includes some words rarely heard today

peremptory: dictatorial

arbitrary: wilful in imposing her opinions on others

a Liberal weekly called The Speaker: This indicates Stephen's political and social outlook: progressive in his opinions but shocked by socialist views. Many of Shaw's plays contain attacks on supporters of the Liberal Party, which reached the height of its power in the half century from 1868 to the eve of the first world war

let that chain alone: Stephen is nervously playing with his watch chain. Shaw gives a sly hint of the 'tie' and 'chain' by which his mother limits his freedom

Only a —: Stephen's amazement testifies to the overwhelming impression Lady Britomart makes on others. This is useful guidance to the actress playing the role

Harrow and Cambridge: Stephen has had a typical upper-class education

his trustees: his legal guardians since his father's death

as poor as church mice: a traditional simile implying extreme poverty, certainly an exaggeration here. Shaw gives information later in the play, which casts light on the value of eight hundred pounds in 1906; the thirty-eight shillings a week (approximately a hundred pounds a year) that Andrew Undershaft will pay a workman is regarded as a good wage

Barbara: the name of the patron saint of gunners and miners. See Commentary, pp. 66–7, on the legend of St Barbara

the Salvation Army: a Christian organisation founded in 1865 (and named in 1878) by William Booth (1829–1912) to combine missionary work with social welfare work in the slums of the great cities, first in England, then in many other countries of the world. The organisation still continues and is highly respected

We are Whigs: Whigs and Tories formed the two great political parties in England after 1689. During the nineteenth century, the name 'Whig' was largely replaced by 'Liberal', but continued sometimes to be applied to Liberals of old-fashioned views, clearly distinguished from their Radical allies. The term recalls the Whig Oligarchy, the group of wealthy and powerful families that was the real government of England for a large part of the eighteenth century.

Stevenage: an actual 'new town' which is within easy reach of London (see Commentary, p. 75). The title given to Stephen's grandfather is an anticipation of the garden city provided for the workers in his father's arms factory

give up society: stop engaging in the expensive life of the upper class; 'society' was snobbishly used to mean only the fashionable leisure class
fabulously wealthy: the adverb is appropriate to wealth as inexhaustible as we hear of in fairy tales
the Woolwich Infant: the name of a cannon. Woolwich Arsenal was the central storehouse of ammunition for the British Army
get up revivals: organise mass religious re-awakenings
Lazarus: a Jewish name. Shaw's use of it reflects a common association of Jewish financiers with big business, but it is ironical that Lazarus is the name of the poor man in the story told in the Bible (St Luke 16) to which Shaw alludes in the Preface. There is another biblical Lazarus, whom Christ miraculously raised from the dead (St John 11–12), as Barbara in Act III is raised from despair and the death of her old life to new life and hope
kowtowed to: showed excessive respect to; from a Chinese gesture of worship
Bismarck: Otto Eduard Leopold von Bismarck (1815–98), the powerful Chancellor of the German Empire from 1871 to 1890
Gladstone: William Ewart Gladstone (1809–98), the leading British Liberal statesman of the nineteenth century; he was Prime Minister from 1868 to 1874 and 1880 to 1885, again in 1886, and finally from 1892 to 1894
Disraeli: Benjamin Disraeli (1804–81), the leader of the Tory Party and Prime Minister from 1867 to 1868 and from 1874 to 1880
Lord Chamberlain: a ceremonial court appointment which entailed a real power of censorship over the theatre, not abolished until 1968
declare war on the Sultan. They wouldnt: probably a reference to Disraeli's avoidance of war with Turkey after the savage Turkish suppression of disturbances in Bulgaria in 1875 and 1876, when Russia seized the excuse to send troops into the area
broke the law when he was born: it is later revealed that his illegitimate birth was the essential qualification for winning the Undershaft inheritance
a foundling: Shaw's primary use of the term is to indicate simply an illegitimate child; but it is probable that he also wanted to suggest an association with 'the foundling

of Euripidean tragedy who turns out to be the son of a god and inherits a kingdom' (Gilbert Murray, 'Excursus on the Ritual Forms Preserved in Greek Tragedy', in Jane Harrison, *Themis*, new edition, Meridian Books, Cleveland, 1962, p. 341)

the parish of St Andrew Undershaft: the old church of St Andrew Undershaft stands in the City (the financial centre) of London. It is supposed to have got its name from the fact that its steeple was not as high as the maypole (shaft) set up annually on May Day opposite the south doorway before the reign of Henry VIII. However, Undershaft as a character's name is comparable to Shotover in Shaw's later play, *Heartbreak House*, and 'shaft' can mean 'arrow', 'missile', or alternatively 'pit' or 'underground tunnel', both appropriate to the subversive attack that Undershaft is to make on the ideals of Cusins and Barbara

Stuff: shortened form of 'Stuff and nonsense!', an expression of impatience with foolishness

the Roman Empire under the Antonines: Antoninus Pius, Roman Emperor from AD 138 to 161, had been adopted by the Emperor Hadrian, and he in turn adopted Marcus Aurelius and Lucius Verus who became emperors after him. Edward Gibbon (1737–94) begins *The Decline and Fall of the Roman Empire* (1776–88) with an account of the flourishing of Roman culture in the period of the Antonines

a Pharisee: a member of an ancient Jewish sect who prided themselves on strict observance of the Law; hence used of any self-righteous person, often implying hypocrisy as well

a sort of religion of wrongness: this charge against Undershaft links the character with one of Shaw's acknowledged masters, William Blake (1757–1827), who attacked the evils of conventional Christianity and the social system it supported, in poems and prophetic books which invert accepted values. 'The Vision of Christ that thou dost see/Is my vision's greatest enemy', Blake wrote in *The Everlasting Gospel*, and again: 'Both read the Bible day and night,/But thou read'st black where I read white'. See Commentary, p. 76

Bedford Square ... Hampstead: very good addresses for well-to-do professional people

a farthing: a coin, now obsolete, worth only a quarter of one penny

the money is settled: Undershaft has made a legal arrangement for Lady Britomart to receive regularly the money needed to support her household and bring up the children from a large sum permanently set aside for the purpose

a question of how much: apart from the light this sheds on the practical, or unprincipled, nature of Lady Britomart's morality, it is Shaw's simplest statement of one of the play's chief themes: What is the price of a human soul?

put my pride in my pocket: set aside my pride

it fidgets me: the more familiar usage is 'it makes me fidget', or 'it makes me uneasy'

your countenance: your moral support; Shaw's choice of word carries the implication that it is for show (the look of it) only that Lady Britomart wants Stephen's approval

cows me: intimidates me

where she picked it up: Lady Britomart's real or assumed unawareness of the impression she makes is an important stroke of characterisation

mundane: belonging to the fashionable world; perhaps also 'worldly' in contrast to Barbara's spiritual quality

man about town: upper-class man of fashion and leisure; a term normally applied to bachelors

Lomax's complaint: Shaw means 'a frivolous sense of humor'

swains: an archaic word generally applied to rustic youths (usually in artificial, pastoral literature), not to sophisticated urban types

Dolly: this affectionate diminutive recalls Shaw's response to the view of marriage given by Ibsen in *A Doll's House* (1879): that 'it is the man who is the doll'

Ripping: (*Edwardian slang*) excellent, splendid

'Onward Christian Soldiers': a very popular hymn by Sabine Baring-Gould (1834–1924) sung to a marching tune

a bit thick: slang understatement, implying 'excessive', 'outrageous'

with ominous suavity: Shaw requires the actress to suggest Lady Britomart's irritation through a deliberately polite manner. The character is made more interesting by such indications that her manner may be a concealing mask all the time

Homer: Greek epic poet, known as author of *The Iliad* and *The Odyssey*, believed to have lived about 900BC

Autolycus:	a figure from Greek mythology, son of Hermes, grandfather of Odysseus, and an expert thief and trickster, whose name was borrowed by Shakespeare (1564–1616) for the pedlar described as 'a snapper-up of unconsidered trifles' in *The Winter's Tale*. The phrase Cusins quotes comes from *The Iliad*, X, line 267. Although the first word may indeed be translated as 'thick' (the whole phrase refers to a well-stocked house), Cusins's rendering is a bit of a joke which Shaw undoubtedly owed to Gilbert Murray. See Commentary, pp. 73–4
Tush:	an exclamation dismissing the topic and the speaker as not worth serious attention
kid:	this slang word for 'child' is an accepted colloquialism in many circles, even middle-class and upper-class, today, though it is still not standard English
a regular corker:	slang expression: 'regular' is here an intensifier (like 'real', or 'considerable'); 'corker' is applied to something or someone that arrests attention, or unanswerably stops dispute
The—er—:	Morrison is about to announce 'The master', then checks himself
Notatall:	running the three words together is an indication of Lomax's slangy way of speaking
Takes you... dont it:	It takes you... doesn't it
really you know, upon my soul!:	disconnected exclamations are typical of Lomax's style of speaking
a dissenter:	a nonconformist in religion who rejects the authority of the Church of England
not your sort of blood and fire:	Lomax regards the Salvation Army motto as entirely metaphorical; Undershaft responds by claiming that literal killing and devastation can bring spiritual benefits. Much the same claim was to be made by the poet Rupert Brooke (1887–1915) in the sonnets he wrote at the outbreak of the First World War
Mile End:	in the East End of London, one of the poorer quarters
tosh:	(*Edwardian slang*) nonsense
conscience money:	here simply money given to ease one's conscience; but see note on the Preface, p. 61
Christmas card moralities:	childishly sentimental moral views. Undershaft by implication is dismissing the traditional Christmas message of 'Peace on earth'

24 · Summaries

resist not evil, and turn the other cheek: Christ's precepts in the Bible (St Matthew 5:39), often quoted in support of the pacifist cause

overtaxed: mentally overstrained

As Euripides says ...: the common English proverb voiced by Cusins roughly sums up the moral of *The Bacchae* of Euripides (480–406BC) in which the power of the god Dionysos is shown to be double-edged, potentially life-enhancing or maddening and death-bringing

Bosh!: (*slang*) meaning 'worthless stuff', often used as an exclamation with rather comic effect

infidels: unbelievers; generally used of those who subscribe to another religion than Christianity, but rarely heard today

the sign of the cross: Barbara unquestioningly accepts the symbol that Shaw himself associates with an aspect of Christianity he regards as false and vicious (see the Preface on 'Crosstianity'). The original audience would have been reminded of a popular melodrama, *The Sign of the Cross* (1896) by Wilson Barrett (died 1904)

Canning Town: an industrial area in the East End of London

Perivale St Andrews. At the sign of the sword: the names of many English villages refer to the saint to whom the parish church is dedicated, so the Undershaft religion is recognised in the name of the town dominated by the armament works. The sword, although a conventional symbol of warfare, is not in simple opposition to the Christian sign of the cross, if Christ's words are recalled: 'I came not to send peace, but the sword' (St Matthew 10:34) – implying active heroism rather than passive suffering

Thourt passing: 'Thou art passing', 'passing' being a euphemism for 'dying'

get saved: Evangelical Christianity stressed the need for the individual to make a deliberate choice of salvation after a period of spiritual agony

ring for prayers: a formal service of family prayers, conducted by the head of the household and attended by everyone, servants included, was regularly held in many respectable upper and middle-class households in the nineteenth century

for a lark: (*slang*) meaning 'for fun', or in more modern idiom, 'for kicks'

keep your countenance: a less formal equivalent would be 'keep a straight face'

we have done things... no health in us: taken from the General Confession in the Church of England service of Evening Prayer

humbug me: deceive me, fool me

tell on me: betray me by telling the facts; Cusins is playfully using child's language here

a sudden flounce: a quick movement expressing disdain

Act II

The first section of Act II presents happenings at the West Ham Shelter the next day, before Undershaft's arrival. Snobby Price, Rummy Mitchens and Peter Shirley represent the frauds who pretend to be converted in order to benefit from the Salvation Army's charity, and the genuine unfortunates who are helped irrespective of their religious views. Bill Walker arrives in search of his girl-friend who has joined the 'Army'. His violence terrifies the spongers and the young Salvation lass, Jenny Hill, whom he hits in the face. However, Barbara handles him confidently and shrewdly, undermining his self-respect. Undershaft arrives and silently watches Barbara's efforts to awaken Bill Walker's moral sense. When Cusins enters, Barbara draws him into the discussion with Bill, who now decides to flee from her nagging and seek physical punishment at the hands of a converted wrestler, Todger Fairmile. Cusins and Undershaft are left together. Though they are soon arguing about religious values and social virtues, they reach a mutual understanding from which Barbara is excluded. Cusins sees that Undershaft will be cunning and unscrupulous in his attempt to detach his daughter from the Salvation Army. He is himself amused, revolted and impressed by Undershaft's views, but makes no attempt to oppose his course of action; instead, Cusins observes Undershaft's dealings with Barbara as the older man had watched her dealings with Bill Walker. The others return from a meeting at the far gate of the shelter and count the money they have collected. Undershaft offers to add a small contribution, but Barbara will not accept the tainted money he has made from his murderous business. Bill now returns and tells how Todger Fairmile turned him into a laughing-stock, without satisfying his wish for justice to clear him of guilt. So he tries to clear himself by getting Jenny, or the Army, to accept compensation from the money he has saved. Barbara again insists that money will not buy spiritual things, and she resists the temptation her father puts before her: that he will give ninety-nine pounds if she accepts Bill's one pound. Mrs Baines, the Salvation Army Commissioner, has no such scruples. Fund-raising is her business and she has good news to announce: that Lord Saxmundham has promised to give five thousand pounds to keep the shelter open through the winter, if an equal amount can be got from other wealthy gentlemen. This is Undershaft's opportunity. He writes out a cheque for the full amount, and it is accepted by Mrs Baines with rejoicing. Except for Barbara, Bill Walker and Peter Shirley, all the people in the shelter march off to a great meeting, with Cusins beating the drum and Undershaft playing the trombone. The Army's acceptance of Undershaft's cheque has released Bill from his awe of a superior moral standard. His independence and scepticism are strengthened when he finds that Snobby Price has stolen his sovereign.

NOTES AND GLOSSARY:

warehouse: converted from commerce to its present charitable use by the Salvation Army

horse-trough: London's roads were still full of horse-drawn traffic at this time, but Shaw's inclusion of this visual detail, symmetrically balancing the table, is too striking to be simply realistic: it hints that the poor are being fed like working animals here

penthouse: a shelter with a sloping roof

takes a pull at: drinks from

arter: represents Cockney (London East End) pronunciation of 'after'. (Standard and phonetic spelling alternated in the speeches of Cockney characters in the 1907 edition of *Major Barbara*. Shaw made the change to full phonetic spelling in 1931, and this was kept in subsequent editions)

praps: vulgar pronunciation of 'perhaps'

wot: what

workin: working

Yus, I dessay: Yes, I dare say

nothink: nothing; pronouncing -ing as -ink was a common vulgarism

isself: his self (more correctly 'himself')

thirty-eight bob: 'bob' is a slang term for a shilling (now the five pence piece) and may be plural, as here, or singular; the sum given here is nearly two pounds

Fust: First

fffff!: he shivers

station ... call me: a variant on a line in the Catechism of the Church of England, printed in the Prayer Book: 'to do my duty in that state of life, unto which it shall please God to call me'. See below, pp. 33 and 78

through em:	'em' is an old pronoun form (modern 'them') surviving in the colloquial English of some areas
bein:	being; compare 'meetins' for 'meetings' below; there are several other examples of this careless pronunciation in the text
doo:	due
appiness:	happiness
somethink cruel:	vulgar for 'terribly', 'very hard'
chawnce:	chance
so's to leave arf... me:	so as to leave half... my
fly:	(*slang*) sharp, knowing
pinch:	(*slang*) steal
me ands:	my hands
do as the Romans do:	a common saying, originally the advice of St Ambrose (AD337–97) to St Augustine (AD354–430)
rotten:	simply intensifies 'bad'; vulgar speech
carpenter:	contributes to a trail of references whereby Barbara's experiences are associated with Christ's (brought up as the son of a carpenter)
uppish:	cheeky
a Chartist:	a supporter of the People's Charter, a programme of political reform, between 1837 and 1848. Chartism was mainly a working-class movement and a forerunner of socialism in Britain
a stationer:	a tradesman who sells writing materials, traditionally involved with printing and book-selling
hewers of wood and drawers of water:	biblical terms for manual workers taken from the Book of Joshua 9:21
Your elth:	Price imitates the manners of gentlemen drinking a lady's health in wine
Missis:	the spelling is a conventional indication of vulgar speech, though it represents the normal standard pronunciation of 'Mrs'
gittin:	getting, arranging to be
a bad un:	a bad one, old-fashioned vulgarism for a wicked, immoral person
they likes:	they like; grammatically incorrect
av a bit o credit:	have a bit of credit, get recognition of merit
if we was to let on:	if we were to admit
Wish I ad:	I wish I had
Romola:	the heroine of a novel of that name, set in Renaissance Italy, by George Eliot (Mary Ann Evans, 1819–80)
Both on us:	Both of us

28 · Summaries

nobody cawnt: nobody can; Price uses the non-standard double negative ('no... n[o]t'); compare 'dont... no more' below
wopped: (*slang*) beat
Billy and Sally wasnt: grammatically incorrect; compare 'confessions is' and 'what you done' below
be er: by her
an lam into er: and thrash her; 'lam' is a word of Norse origin, now only rarely used, in colloquial English or dialect
az: has
wispered: the difference in pronunciation between this and 'whispered' would be very slight
spose: suppose
blokes: (*slang*) men
I'll take it out in gorspellin: I'll compensate (myself) for it by enjoying gospel meetings, or preaching the gospel. This is a minor example of the association of religious enthusiasm with the effects of alcohol, both providing a release from sober rationality
pluck up: shortened form of 'pluck up your courage'; compare 'cheer up'
appiness ere: happiness here
Ere: Here
buck up, daddy!: pull yourself together, old man; another expression of encouragement
fetchin y'a thick slice o breadn treacle: fetching you a thick slice of bread and treacle
skyblue: watery milk; an unfamiliar usage today
art: heart
pennorth: penny-worth
jawrin: jawing, nagging
ony: only
jumped-up: usually applied to someone who has risen rather suddenly in society and behaves arrogantly; but Price cares for the sound of words more than their meaning
jerked-off: perhaps 'turned out of doors', or 'dismissed from his job'
orspittle-turned-out: this compound word is Shaw's invention, and his use of it helps characterise Price. It seems to mean 'turned out by the hospital', perhaps because he is too ill to be helped
Make the thievin swine ... from you: Price seems to identify the Salvation Army with the capitalist employers

Awsk a blessin: Ask a blessing, say a prayer before eating
tuck that into you: get that inside you, eat that
lovey: a Cockney endearment, 'little love'
the piece that I value more: Price's pun on the identically sounding 'piece' (of bread) and 'peace' is another demonstration of his cleverness with words
peace that passeth hall hannerstennin: peace that passeth all understanding; a liturgical formula quoted from the Prayer Book, part of the blessing with which the priest dismisses the congregation at the end of a service
a rough customer: a set phrase in which 'customer' means 'person one has to deal with'
Aw knaow you ... In you gow: I know you. You're the one that took away my girl. You're the one that set her against me. Well, I'm going to have her out. Not that I care a curse for her or you: see? But I'll let her know; and I'll let you know. I'm going to give her a doing [a beating] that'll teach her to cut away from me. Now in with you and tell her to come out afore [before] I come in and kick her out. Tell her Bill Walker wants her. She'll know what that means; and if she keeps me waiting it'll be worse. You stop to jaw back at me [answer me back]; and I'll start on you: do you hear? There's your way. In you go
Oo ... callin mate: Who ... calling mate (friend)
aint doin ... no arm: isn't doing ... any harm
Youre gowin ... ends: You're going to stand up for her, are you? Put up your hands; Bill is inviting Price to fight him with his fists
Gawd forgive you: a mocking imitation of Jenny's words
Ev you ... agen it?: Have you anything to say against it?
Good job for you!: You are lucky
Aw'd pat: I'd put
fawt: fight
stawved: starved
em Aw: am I
fice: face
Mijor: Major
downt: don't
nao: no
shaow ... thet: show ... that
lawk: like
to cam: to come
Eah: Here

30 · Summaries

your mess:	your meal; still used in the Armed Forces for a group that eats together (as in 'the officers' mess'), it is in origin the same word as 'mass', the sanctified ritual meal of the Catholic Church
git ... wy:	get out of my way
take a liberty with:	insult, take advantage of
aold palsy mag:	old palsy mug; 'mug' is here a slang term for 'fool', and 'palsy' is a comment on Shirley's frail physique
soaker:	heavy drinker
give ... and happy ... sure:	the condensed style gives greater vividness as it suggests a dramatic exchange, with Bill impersonating the employer whose words he uses
a character:	a testimonial, or written recommendation of character
the differ:	the difference; colloquialism rarely heard today
beeyave:	behave
layin:	laying; only in a few expressions does 'lay' denote a violent action (as in 'lay on', here 'lay across')
Downt provowk ... eah:	Don't provoke me to lay it across yours: do you hear
I aint:	I haven't
loy:	lie
soupkitchener:	one who receives free soup from a charitable organisation
You ... you:	this repetition of the subject pronoun gives an aggressive rhythm to the sentence
yang menn eah:	young man here
itt:	hit
crosseyed:	squinting; applied to a thief, the term suggests glances made in all directions to spot valuables to be picked up
loafer:	idler
Oo's ee?:	Who is he?
Todger:	'to todge' was a verb in country use meaning 'smash to pulp'
Balls Pond:	a district in north London
Him:	more emphatic than 'He' in colloquial usage
wrastler:	wrestler
awl:	the spelling distinguishes Bill's broader Cockney accent from Peter Shirley's; so with 'cawnt' below
Ken:	Can
thet you sy:	that you say
stend ap to anny menn alawv:	stand up to any man alive
perfeshnal:	professional, here one who fights for money

wouldnt a:	wouldn't have
teetotaller:	one who drinks no alcohol
oald lawr:	old liar
blooming:	Cockney expletive intensifying 'good'
awdin:	hiding; beating
Aw lawk to ev:	I like to have
a bit o devil:	a touch of fighting spirit. Bill makes a commonplace association between drink and the devil which anticipates the linking of Bodger (the whisky distiller) and Undershaft ('Prince of Darkness') later in Act II
An eah Aw emm:	And here I am
blawter:	blighter; slang term for a man who is a nuisance
sted o:	instead of
givin her wot for:	giving her what she deserves; implying physical punishment
station:	police station
Garn!:	Go on! A vulgar expression of incredulity
jastice ... cantry:	justice ... country
them people:	those people, the aristocracy
coroner's inquest:	legal investigation of a death that may have been suicide or the effect of dangerous industrial work
the knackers:	those whose business is the buying and slaughtering of worn-out horses
Secularist:	one who believes that morality should relate solely to the well-being of humanity on earth. Secularism was promulgated by G. J. Holyoake (1817–1906)
chawge:	(*legal*) charge
Moy nime's:	My name is
wot call as she:	what reason has she
pluck:	courage
kentin:	canting, tiresomely pious
spowse:	suppose
demmiged:	damaged
downt:	don't
bread and scripe:	bread and scrape, bread spread very sparingly with butter
ketlep:	cat-lap, milk
blieve:	believe
a slight:	mild insult
alown:	alone
enaff:	enough
Awve ed:	I've had
maw gel:	my girl

tike her aht o this:	take her out of this
brike er jawr:	break her jaw
get shut:	get rid; colloquial
tangue:	tongue, figuratively used for 'talk'
fawnd:	find
beck:	back
do two years for you:	Bill is willing to serve a prison sentence for assault on Barbara
face clean and hair washed:	'Cleanliness is next to godliness' was a common saying; Barbara associates ordinary secular improvements with spiritual conversion
Wottud:	What did
carroty slat:	slut with carrot-coloured hair
put your nose out of joint:	given you cause for jealousy
carse:	curse
mawnd:	mind
judy:	girl's name, used colloquially to refer to any girl
iz:	his
bleedin:	bleeding; a swear word, like 'bloody'
He's gev em up:	He has given them up
wight:	weight
Thirteen four:	thirteen stones, four pounds (84.38 kg)
e can lick me:	he can defeat me
She's dan me:	she's beaten me
av the lor of:	have the law of; bring a legal charge against
flateared pignosed potwalloper:	like Price, Rummy is a skilful inventor of colourful phrases; 'potwalloper' is a slang term for a kitchen boy
hintroduced:	Rummy, imitating upper-class talk and anxious not to drop her aitches, puts one in the wrong place
lea me alown:	leave me alone
a mischief:	an injury
ennywy:	anyway
afeerd:	old form of 'afraid', surviving in colloquial English or dialect
prime company:	excellent company
Whats kep:	What has kept
lasses:	the usual term for girls in Salvation Army uniform who are not officers
outpatient:	a humorous reference to Bill, sitting apart and looking sick, as if he was waiting at a hospital for treatment
taold:	told
***devil-may-care*:**	carefree

eppy enaff:	happy enough
Woy cawnt you lea me alown:	Why can't you leave me alone
ev I dan:	have I done
Ev dan wiv it:	Have done with it, stop talking, that's enough
Chack it:	Chuck it; make an end of it
Dont lets get you cheap:	the theme of the value of the individual soul emerges again
a awt:	a heart
sime:	same
neggin and provowkin:	nagging and provoking
merry im:	marry him
Gawd elp im:	God help him
Awve aony ... lawftawm:	I've only had to stand it for a morning: he'll have to stand it for a lifetime
beshed:	bashed
an nar Aw'll:	and now I'll
cam beck:	come back
shaow:	show
ardern:	harder than
mike us square:	make us even; Bill's idea of justice is based on equality
genlmn:	gentleman
oughter knaow:	ought to know
awst:	asked
mahth shat:	mouth shut
nao sach a thing:	no such thing
saoul:	soul
Ah kin you tell wevver:	How can you tell whether
sathink:	something
urtin:	hurting
tike maw tip:	take my tip, follow my advice
mite:	mate; he addresses Cusins as an equal
doy afoah your tawm:	die before your time
Wore aht:	Worn out
rataplan:	onomatopoeic word for a drumming noise, a tattoo
Church Catechism:	the basic teachings of the Church of England in the form of question-and-answer, included in the Book of Common Prayer
Baptism and—:	the statement in the Prayer Book continues with: 'the Supper of the Lord', referring to the sacrament of Holy Communion, corresponding to the mass in the Catholic Church
hell-ridden evangelical sects:	Protestant sects preaching fear of hell as the means to conversion

a sally: a sudden rush; used in military contexts
the Highest: this form of reference to God should be remembered when Barbara refers to her 'rank' near the end of Act III
rhapsodist: reciter of poems, especially the Homeric poems, in ancient Greece; modern uses imply an excited, inspired manner
Dionysos: also called Bacchus, Greek god of wine and the forces of nature; the name was used by Nietzsche in *The Birth of Tragedy* (see p. 70) to symbolise a radical challenge to Christian morality
dithyrambs: choric hymns in honour of Dionysos
Euripides: Euripides (480–406BC) was one of the three great tragic dramatists of ancient Greece. Gilbert Murray specialised in translations of his plays (see pp. 69, 73)
One and another . . . : from Murray's translation of *The Bacchae* by Euripides
Methodists: widespread dissenting sects which emerged out of the Church of England in the eighteenth century, generally more puritanical and commonly of lower social class than the membership of the State Church
Calvinism: the protestant theology of John Calvin (1509–64) is marked by determinism (hateful to Shaw), representing men as predestined to be saved or damned. Calvin's ideal city at Geneva was ruled by a tyrannical puritanism
Presbyterianism: a non-hierarchical system of church government by a body of priests or elders
the Undershaft inheritance: a paradoxical name for originality
mad as a hatter: nineteenth-century proverbial phrase of obscure origin
Colossus — Mammoth: these hyperbolic terms (originally signifying a gigantic statue and a kind of elephant) contribute to an impression of Undershaft as superhuman
St Francis: St Francis of Assisi (about 1181–1226), founder of the religious brotherhood of Friars Minor, whose members refused possessions and lived a wandering existence, preaching faith in Christ; in modern times the best loved of Christian saints
St Simeon: Simeon Salus (*d.*?590), a Syrian who devoted himself to caring for outcasts and the very poorest people

draws their teeth:	renders them harmless. The following passage imitates the stylistic device known as stichomythia in ancient Greek drama
their shop:	(*slang*) their job
Trade Unionism nor Socialism:	Undershaft's viewpoint is quite distinct from the dramatist's here
infernal:	the primary association with the mythical Lower Regions, or hell, is combined with colloquial usage as a semi-humorous expletive
elp to keep hathers stright:	help to keep others straight
The millionaire's mite:	a reference to the story of the two mites that Christ observed the poor widow give to the treasury of the temple (St Mark 12:41–4). Two mites were worth one quarter of a penny, but 'she of her want did cast in all she had, even all her living'
patent Grand Duke hand grenade:	it was a hand grenade that killed Grand Duke Sergius, mentioned in the Preface
good blood can cleanse them:	a reference to the redemptive power of the blood Christ had shed
a caution:	humorous expression applied to someone or something extraordinary; slang of American origin
a Cheap Jack:	an auctioneer, especially one who sells off goods at fairs, or in the street. In this phrase, 'cheap' is an old word for a bargain
Mile End Waste:	an open-air market on waste land in the East End of London
Mephistopheles:	name of the devil who in the legend of Faust, is the scholar-hero's guide and companion, fulfilling all his wishes on earth in return for his soul. Already in the play *Doctor Faustus* (1604) by Christopher Marlowe (1564–93) this devil shows a spiritual awareness that Faustus lacks until death is upon him; in the *Faust* (Part I, 1808; Part II, 1832) of Johann Wolfgang von Goethe (1749–1832) Mephistopheles is an ironical *alter ego*, or second self of Faustus. See Commentary, pp. 75–6
Machiavelli:	Niccolo Machiavelli (1467–1527), the Italian author of *The Prince* (1532), a classic treatise on the art of government. Machiavelli advocated total realism (what came to be known as *realpolitik*) including reliance on 'force and fraud' in handling men, as essential to strong government. This shocked all who professed Christian sentiments, even though they might accept Machiavellian methods in

	practice as necessary evils in the pursuit of particular ends. Compare Shaw's remarks on cynics in the Preface
dad:	Barbara has quickly become on familiar terms with her father. The Devil is traditionally, rather humorously, referred to as 'old dad'

like a cleaned-out gambler: another occurrence of the motif of the bet, or bid

Bin talkin ever sence:	You've been talking ever since
Nao e aint:	No, he hasn't
from orf:	a vulgarism equivalent to 'off'
the grahnd in Pawkinses Corner:	the ground in Parkins's Corner
rabbed orf be maw shaoulders:	rubbed off by my shoulders
sivin:	saving
tawm:	time
prying camfortable wiv me as a cawpet:	praying comfortably with me as a carpet
the aol bloomin meetin:	the whole blooming meeting. See note on 'bloomin', p. 31 above
sez:	says; the spelling represents the normal standard pronunciation
Ow Lawd brike is stabborn sperrit:	Oh, Lord, break his stubborn spirit
bat downt urt is dear art:	but don't hurt his dear heart
blowk:	bloke
Fanny:	Funny
ap at the skoy:	up at the sky
Ow...fahnd:	Oh...found
Glaory Allelloolier:	Glory Halleluia
Braddher:	Brother
dahned:	downed, laid down
me mather worshin me a Setterda nawt:	my mother washing me on Saturday night
Aw ednt jast nao shaow wiv im:	I hadn't just no show with him; I didn't have any chance with him, it wasn't a fight at all
the tather arf larfed:	the tother half laughed; 'the tother' is a surviving dialect form for 'the second', 'the other'; not confined to Cockney
theirselves:	themselves
settisfawd nah:	satisfied now
wish:	colloquial for 'I wish'
hextra:	extra
browk:	broke
be forgive:	vulgarism for 'be forgiven'
py:	pay

trawd to gat:	tried to get
Tell y'Aw:	I tell you I
being mide ... my pines:	being made a sight of in the public street for my pains
wy:	way
quid:	(*slang*) a pound (£1)
sived agen the frost:	saved against the frost; 'agin' here means 'in readiness for', 'in defence against'; extra money would be needed for coals in very cold weather
gowing to merry:	going to marry
fawnd:	fined – by a magistrate for assault
a rawt to itt er:	a right to hit her; assuming what was then a husband's legal power over his wife
fawv:	five
manney:	money
dan and pide:	done and paid; 'done' in the sense of finished with
lawkly:	likely
ev the lawr o me:	have the law on me, bring a charge against me
mach:	much
mawt:	might
gime:	game
wownt ev plyed agen me:	won't have played against me
mikes a menn:	makes a man
iz lawf's a burdn to im:	his life's a burden to him
thraowin:	throwing
beshed fice:	bashed face
hap:	up
grendorter:	grand-daughter
anderd:	hundred
the standard price to buy anybody who's for sale:	Barbara is alluding to the betrayal of Christ by his faithless disciple, Judas Iscariot, for thirty pieces of silver; but it can also be said that Christ was bought for this money. The idea that the good, as well as the evil, can be bought, or may sell themselves, anticipates Cusins's remarks in Act III: 'It is not the sale of my soul that troubles me...'
awtful tangued:	artful tongued
sovereign:	gold coin, now obsolete, worth £1
Pall Mall:	an imposing street in the West End of London
ome:	home
Mansion House:	the official residence of the Lord Mayor of London, elected head of the banking and commercial community

38 · Summaries

A new creation: a title recently given; perhaps also suggesting that Bodger is a new man, his soul saved
Wot prawce selvytion nah?: What price salvation now? A key line
in letters of fire: neon lighting for advertisements was a new invention when Shaw wrote *Major Barbara*; 'fire', in Barbara's phrase, has associations with hell
tied houses: public houses owned by a brewery or distillery, or obliged to sell liquor supplied by a particular firm
Rotten dranken: the past participle of the verb 'to drink' (usually 'drunken') here means 'when it is drunk' or 'for drinking'
lyddite: a high explosive, first tested at Lydd in Kent
egg on: urge on
peace... and good will to men: spoken by the angel announcing Christ's birth to the shepherds (in the Bible, St Luke 2:14)
an Olympian diapason: a burst of harmony such as might be heard on Olympus, the home of the Greek gods
Zion: originally the hill in Palestine on which the city of King David was built, but commonly used in reference to heaven
vamp a bass: improvise a bass part to accompany the melody
one of Donizetti's operas: Gaetano Donizetti's (1797–1848) *Lucia di Lammermoor* (1835), based on a novel by Sir Walter Scott (1771–1832). The wedding march is an ironic contrast to Lucia's distraught emotions in the opera, as it is to Barbara's emotions here
Dionysos Undershaft has descended: like the god who appears among his worshippers in human form. Cusins in this scene can be described in actors' slang as 'camping it up', indulging in comic exaggeration. By this means Shaw makes what happens at the shelter seem like supernatural events in a mythic action
'My ducats and my daughter': quoted from Shylock, the Jew in Shakespeare's *The Merchant of Venice*, whose daughter runs away with a Christian, taking a large sum of money with her
My God: why hast thou forsaken me?: One of the last sayings attributed to Christ dying on the cross (St Matthew 27:46, St Mark 15:34)
wen aw wiz dahn: when I was down
Waw: why
Ellow: Hullo
summun else ez: someone else has
Weres it gorn: Where has it gone

Bly me:	a Cockney exclamation of amazement, usually spelt 'Blimey'
Stowl:	Stole
macker:	mucker, a scavenger
serve you art:	serve you out
y'pahnd:	your pound
paean:	a cry of triumph; in ancient Greece, a hymn of thanksgiving for victory
I done you:	I've tricked you, or simply, I've defeated you
Ive ad it aht o y—:	I've had it out of y—
cawnt baw:	can't buy
rahnd:	round
aw rawt:	all right
pasnl:	personal
Sao long:	So long; a colloquial expression of leave-taking
Cleaned out:	bankrupt, destitute
a Rowton doss:	a bed in a common lodging house. Lord Rowton (1838–1903) was chairman of a charitable organisation which provided shelter for the homeless
Tom Paine's books:	principally *The Age of Reason* (1794; 1795; 1807) and *The Rights of Man* (1791–2) by Thomas Paine (1737–1809)
Bradlaugh's lectures:	Charles Bradlaugh (1833–91), a leading humanist, was excluded from Parliament in 1880, because he refused, as an atheist, to take the formal religious oath of loyalty
read . . . in the proper spirit:	this 'curtain line' is specially emphatic because of its position. By making the audience, or reader, think of Tom Paine, secularist, democrat, source of ideas for both the French and the American revolutions at the end of the eighteenth century, the author can prevent the interpretation of his play exclusively in religious terms; the message is secular and political

Act III

This is broken into two parts by a change of setting. The first part again takes place in the library at Wilton Crescent, where Lady Britomart, her children and Charles Lomax gather before setting off for the munitions works. Barbara is no longer wearing her uniform. Cusins arrives late, having taken the morning to recover from a drinking bout in Undershaft's company. Undershaft himself comes to collect them all, and Lady Britomart tries without success to persuade him to make

Stephen his heir; but Stephen rebels against his mother's interference. Undershaft concludes that Stephen is best fitted for a career in politics, though he insists that it is the capitalists and masters of industry like himself who really determine the policies governments carry out. He tells Barbara and Cusins about his model town, and he stirs Barbara out of her mood of despair. The second part of the Act is set on a slope overlooking the town, a place where the explosives are tested. The tour is over, the visitors are enthusiastic about everything they have seen and a group discussion takes up the remainder of the play. It turns on the question of whether the Undershaft inheritance is to go to Cusins, and so to Barbara through their marriage. Undershaft engages in a conflict of moral views with Cusins, who makes the crucial decision to join the firm and try to use the power this gives him in order to bring good out of evil. Barbara agrees with this decision, as her father has shown her the true nature of the world where her work needs to be done. At the end of the play, Lady Britomart resumes her dominant role over her children, and Undershaft gives Cusins his first orders.

NOTES AND GLOSSARY:

spoon: kiss and cuddle, or engage in love talk; slang of the period

ownest: very own; an invented endearment

your governor's shop: (*slang*) your father's business

Temperance burgundy: a drink approved by those advocating abstention from alcohol

the Prince of Darkness: when Lucifer (the light-bearing archangel) fell from heaven to rule over hell, he was transformed into Satan, Prince of Darkness

larger loves... than the fireside ones: Shaw was a consistent critic of Victorian England's over-valuation of domesticity

hysteria... madman: further reminders of the vital energy outside the power of reason

its brazen roarings... laughter of the damned: to Cusins's perception, Andrew's presence at the meeting was an ironic mockery of the Salvation Army and its conversions, and pandemonium (hell and its noises) took over

drivel: literally 'dribble', figuratively 'talk like an idiot'; Lomax uses the corresponding noun, meaning 'idiotic nonsense'

out of countenance: put out, embarrassed

When they reach... private secretaryships...: a sudden indication that the character of Lomax is not just a conventional type of wealthy fool, it is also a caricature of a kind of professional politician who never does any serious thinking

has just drove:	has just driven; the grammatical solecism is a reminder that the butler, though his manner is formal, is not an upper-class personage
Biddy:	the affectionate nickname is a sign of human intimacy between Andrew and Lady Britomart; it is also, by its similarity of sound and spelling to the adjective 'biddable', meaning 'docile', an indication that Andrew feels himself to be stronger than his formidable wife
the real Undershaft:	one whose vital energy enables him to control the purely material power in the machinery, making him the master of the industrial process, not its servant
it is not good sense:	Shaw is not writing on the level of fantasy or myth in this scene
Barnardo homes:	homes for orphan children set up by Dr Thomas John Barnardo (1845–1905). These are still in existence
School Board Officer:	the 1870 Act introducing universal primary education throughout Britain set up a system of School Boards to administer its provision
Boards of Guardians:	set up in the middle of the nineteenth century to administer the Poor Laws
lamed for life:	Shaw's limited experience of systematic schooling gave him a lifelong contempt for conventional methods of education
humbugged:	tricked by persuasive talk
go into trade:	Stephen has the traditional disdain of an aristocrat for a middle-class occupation
not trade ... enterprise:	Lady Britomart changes the name to avoid being limited by the conventions of her class
latchkey:	the symbol of coming-of-age
rub it in:	(*slang*) keep repeating it (something disagreeable)
magisterially:	with the air of a judge, or statesman
tickled:	amused
that foolish gabble shop:	Shaw's persistent criticism of the irresponsible way the system of parliamentary democracy was operated in England often echoes the anti-democratic statements of Thomas Carlyle (1795–1881) and contributed to the charge of being pro-Fascist brought against him in the 1930s and since. See p. 12
caucuses:	private meetings of the leaders of a party, commonly before elections, to agree on policy

pay the piper and call the tune: a common saying. Shaw here presents Undershaft as an example of the hidden power of wealthy capitalists which makes a sham of an apparently democratic system

Character: Shaw mocks the nineteenth-century liberal evaluation of moral character, so glibly given by Stephen, but 'character' in this sense remains essential to Cusins if, having learnt Undershaft's lesson, he is to hold his own against the cynical and destructive potential in the older man's views

beggars: a slang expression, playfully applied to people felt to be inferiors; but compare Undershaft's later advice to 'kill' poverty and slavery

getting on: growing older

a guy: a 'fright', something grotesque; derived from the name of Guy Fawkes (1570–1606), annually burnt in effigy on 5 November, for his part in the abortive Catholic plot to blow up Parliament

beautiful hillside town: the hill is in symbolic opposition to the pit (the foundry). (Compare the symbols of the pit and the observatory in Shaw's *Heartbreak House*)

Primitive ... sophisticated: Primitive Methodists split off from the main body of Methodism in 1810, claiming that they were returning to greater purity of doctrine; 'sophisticated' is a joke

Ethical Society: a Humanist organisation started in 1793. As a young man, Shaw had frequented its 'church' in South Place, London

The one thing Jones ... any assertion of social equality: Undershaft describes an efficient version of the prevailing system; this is no socialist Utopia

Avaunt!: an archaic word, used traditionally – especially in old plays – to drive off the devil

***Perivale St Andrews*:** Perivale is an actual place, north-west of London, but Shaw's description is of an imaginary town. In the screen version he calls the area where the characters gather, 'Thundercrest'

emplacement: a platform for guns

firestep: the ledge on which soldiers stand to fire their guns

gatekeeper and timekeeper: it is ironic that the secularist should be in the position of St Peter, keeper of the keys of heaven

brainwork ... isnt used to it: this seems out-of-character, but Peter's unhappiness may be an indication that Undershaft's city is not heaven on earth

the various applications of co-operation: ranging from complete communism as advocated by Robert Owen (1771–1858) to arrangements whereby workmen supplied the capital for their industry, or set up their own stores

news from Manchuria: Russia and Japan were at war over Manchuria when Shaw was writing

'Peace hath her victories...': a line from the sonnet 'To Cromwell' by John Milton (1608–74)

smithereens: small fragments; colloquialism of Irish origin

list slippers: made from the material called 'list' used for selvages of cloth, they enable the wearer to shuffle along noiselessly

I will call in a doctor: to declare him insane, and so incapable of deciding responsibly who is to inherit the property

Labor Church: church of the Labour Movement, the politically conscious grouping of artisans and employees that was to be the foundation of the Labour Party

Morris's words: recalling 'No one's man... I am my own master' from his *The Dream of John Ball*, chapter 1. It does not seem particularly in character for Lady Britomart to speak this line, though William Morris (1834–96) was a wealthy man, and the designs and workmanship he promoted were greatly appreciated by upper-class customers who did not share his Marxist politics. The message itself is a challenge to the hierarchical pecking-order that Undershaft has described

the ten commandments in church: the clauses of the Mosaic Law of the Old Testament were traditionally inscribed in a prominent part of every parish church

Chut!: the dismissive sound is usually represented in print as 'Tut'

Agent General: government representative in Britain

deceased wife's sister: marriage within this degree of relationship was made legal in England in 1907. Shaw altered the screen version accordingly

subterfuge: Cusins admits that his eligibility is based on a sham, complying superficially with the rules governing the inheritance. But the intention of the rules is to find vital genius wherever it may be

casuistry: the branch of ethics concerned with settling particular cases of conscience has often been dismissed as evasive quibbling

44 · Summaries

Done in the eye: slang expression drawn from prize-fighting, implying that Cusins has scored over his opponent
Mac: short for Machiavelli, but also a name commonly applied to a Scotsman, as Jack is to Englishmen. The Scots have a (comic) reputation for being particularly careful of money
a shark: someone greedy and extortionate in money matters
Napoleon... George the Third: England officially proclaimed a trade blockade as part of its war against France in 1793, and prohibited neutral countries from trading with France in 1806
A will of which I am a part: what stirs Barbara in these words is recognition that Undershaft's religion shares a major truth with Christianity. See pp. 54–5 below
morality mongering: making futile conventional distinctions between right and wrong
power: one of the most famous aphorisms about power is Lord Acton's (1834–1902) 'Power tends to corrupt, and absolute power corrupts absolutely'. He went on to say: 'Great men are almost always bad men'. Although this last remark corresponds quite closely to what Shaw says in the Preface with reference to cynics, his whole endeavour in this play is to combat the intellectual rejection of power that the aphorism implies and encourages
Cannes: a seaside town in the south of France
the rock I thought eternal: the orthodox symbol for the Christian Church derived from Christ's words to his disciple Peter (Latin *Petrus*, French *Pierre*, means 'rock'): 'Thou art Peter, and upon this rock I will build my church' (St Matthew 16:18)
tinpot: of poor quality, like a pot made of tin
I fed you and clothed you...: compare the biblical passage (St Matthew 25:35, 36): 'I was an hungred and ye gave me meat... Naked, and ye clothed me...'
the seven deadly sins: defined in Christian tradition as: pride, anger, envy, gluttony, sloth, lust and avarice
firing: fuel for heating
lift... millstones from Man's neck: an adaptation of a biblical phrase attributed to Christ: 'Whoso shall offend one of these little ones which believe in me, it were better for him that a millstone were hanged about his neck, and that he were drowned in the depth of the sea' (St Matthew 18:6)

not fifty genuine professional criminals: if there are many more in the great cities today, Shaw would undoubtedly have accounted for the fact on the grounds that Undershaft's warnings and recommendations have not been heeded. Certainly 'they force us to do away with our own liberties and to organize unnatural cruelties' is as apt today as when Shaw wrote

a tall hat and a chapel sitting: the top hat was respectable Victorian 'Sunday-best' headgear, and a pew reserved for regular attenders at chapel was equally a sign of respectability (and prosperity)

Primrose League: founded in 1883 in honour of Benjamin Disraeli (see p. 20); its aim is to support the Conservative Party

American cloth: oilcloth used as easily cleaned covering

Thou shalt starve ere I starve: the second person singular pronoun and verb form are archaic and suggest biblical style, but the sentiment is startlingly anti-Christian, the usually unspoken creed of individualism

When it is the history of every Englishman . . .: this is an argument for a powerful Trade Union movement in place of the 'damned wantlessness' of the working class, to which Shaw refers in the Preface

I had rather be a thief . . . a murderer . . . the braver and more moral one: excellent examples of the type of paradox commonly regarded as a hall-mark of Shaw's writing: he stands a generally accepted truth on its head to reveal a neglected truth

Kill them: the verb is obviously used metaphorically here, but in Undershaft's next speech, 'until at last they get the courage to kill', it may be taken literally (Parliament sanctions executions and declares wars). See Commentary, pp. 79–80

a certain house in Westminster: Parliament

Turn your oughts into shalls: replace moralising by determination

What does it matter whether they are true . . . if they are true?: a classically neat paradox

cut him: refuse to know him

where the carcase is . . . gathered: now Cholly is quoting the Bible: St Matthew 24:28

ticket: label

The scavenger of misery: an aphorism reminiscent of William Blake's style of thinking, exposing the disreputable underside of a virtue, showing it to exist on the unhappiness of others. See pp. 76–7

ryot:	an Indian peasant
fencing:	not really fighting, but parrying Undershaft's attacks; close in meaning to 'quibbling' here
forgiveness...we must pay our debts:	this echoes and rejects part of the Lord's Prayer, the Christian prayer that Barbara later revises: 'Forgive us our debts' (or 'sins we have committed'), as we forgive our debtors' (or 'those who have sinned against us') (St Matthew 6:12)
the words of Plato:	the allusion is to *The Republic* V, 473: 'There will be no end to the troubles of states, or indeed... of humanity itself, till philosophers become kings in this world, or till those we now call kings and rulers really and truly become philosophers'
tempter... choose:	the tempter is traditionally the devil in one of his aspects (and the Lord's Prayer includes the petition: 'Lead us not into temptation'). There is some similarity between the predicament of Cusins and Barbara standing above Perivale St Andrews and that of Christ, after his forty days' fast in the wilderness: 'the devil, taking him up into an high mountain, shewed unto him all the kingdoms of the world in a moment of time./And the devil said unto him, All this power will I give thee, and the glory of them' (St Luke 4:5-7)
best friend... bravest enemy:	this is Shaw's interpretation of Christ's commandment, 'Love your enemies, bless them that curse you' (St Matthew 5:44); compare 'Opposition is true friendship' (William Blake, *The Marriage of Heaven and Hell*). See p. 76
I hate war:	Gilbert Murray devoted himself to work for the League of Nations as a second career. See p. 74
Are you alluding to me?:	this will raise an easy laugh in performance, enabling the audience to relax after the intellectual tension of the previous scene. This transitional section provides a lull before the further concentrated scene between Barbara and Cusins
Greek to you:	another easy joke
What is all human conduct but... sale of our souls for trifles?:	this speech is the culmination of the Faustian theme that has run through the play. See Commentary, pp. 75-6
it must be spiritual power:	this distinguishes Barbara's aim from that of Cusins, who is concerned with secular government, but his following speech reveals the relationship between their aims

The people must have power: compare the second half of Cusins's next speech. There is no doubt here about the commitment to democracy

give the common man weapons against the intellectual man; although Cusins is referring to the power of education, Shaw is not advocating a meritocracy, as his friend and contemporary H. G. Wells (1866–1946) did. The equality envisaged here is based on the Christian sentiment of the brotherhood of men

when the Turks and Greeks were last at war: the Greeks were defeated in the month-long war of 1896–97 over Crete

My best pupil...: this anecdote relates to Gilbert Murray's pupil H. N. Brailsford who became a war correspondent for the *Daily Chronicle*

Hellas: Greece

Silly baby Dolly: this is more than an expression of affection; it is a sign of Barbara recovering her sense of (motherly) superiority. She now takes back the central role from Cusins

if I could have the wings of a dove...: 'Oh that I had wings like a dove! for then would I fly away, and be at rest', another biblical text: Psalm 55:6. Shaw may be exploiting the Christian use of a dove as symbol of the Holy Spirit, third Person of the Trinity alongside God the Father and God the Son

There is no wicked side: Barbara has reached the stage in her understanding represented in the title of Nietzche's *Beyond Good and Evil* (1886). See pp. 48, 70

middle class... no class: Barbara is not speaking now as the earl's granddaughter, but as a symbolic figure

my father's business: an ambiguous phrase, not simply a reference to the firm of Undershaft and Lazarus, but echoing Christ's words, 'I must be about my Father's business' (St Luke 2:49)

Schumann: Robert Schumann (1810–56), German composer

***transfigured*:** in the manuscript, Shaw left a space here and, when he found the word he wanted, wrote it above. Transfiguration has a religious meaning associated with the vision of Christ's divinity when 'his face did shine as the sun, and his raiment was white as the light' (St Matthew 17:2)

I have got rid of the bribe of bread... woman of my rank: there are a number of echoes of the Lord's Prayer in this passage, but it is a drastic revision of the Prayer

48 · Summaries

let me forgive him: compare the sentence from the celebrated version of *The Rubaiyat* of Omar Khayyam by Edward Fitzgerald (1809–83): 'Man's forgiveness give – and take'
raising of hell to heaven: Shaw originally wrote 'earth to heaven'; by substituting 'hell' for 'earth' he brought the line closer to the title of Blake's *Marriage of Heaven and Hell*. See above, p. 21
the Valley of the Shadow: variation on the biblical phrase, 'the valley of the shadow of death'. 'The Shadow' may be a term for the devil, whose being is entirely negative, a simulation of divinity
She has gone right up into the skies: the figurative expression also suggests an Ascension to heaven; perhaps the Barbara left on stage, who seems now to regress to childishness, is no longer possessed by the divine spirit that has been speaking through her

Preface

First aid to critics

Shaw protests at critics' habitual attribution of the ideas in his works to famous European writers. He does not claim special originality, and accepts that all individual achievements are indebted to predecessors, but he draws attention to the little-publicised British tradition to which he belongs.

NOTES AND GLOSSARY:
Churchwarden: officer of a parish church appointed from the laity, often regarded – from the sixteenth century – as a narrow-minded and ignorant person
Schopenhauer: Arthur Schopenhauer (1788–1860), a pessimistic German philosopher who expounded a subjective idealism and considered oriental religions to be superior to Christianity. His most famous work is *The World as Will and Idea* (1819)
Nietzsche: Friedrich Nietzsche (1844–1900), a highly influential German philosopher who followed Schopenhauer in adopting an anti-Christian view of the world, stressing the power of irrational motivation (which he called 'dionysiac'). Among his best known works are: *The Birth of Tragedy* (1872), *Thus Spake Zarathustra* (1883–85) and *Beyond Good and Evil* (1886)

Ibsen:	See Introduction above, pp. 7–8
Strindberg:	August Strindberg (1849–1912), the leading Swedish dramatist
Tolstoy:	Count Leo Tolstoy (1848–1910), author of the classic Russian novels, *War and Peace* (1863–9) and *Anna Karenina* (1874–6), was also a visionary social reformer, converted in 1879 to a rationalised Christianity. Mahatma Gandhi was among those influenced by Tolstoy's ideas
heresiarch:	founder of a heresy or school of belief opposed to the established orthodoxy
cannot countenance:	cannot look favourably upon
Charles Lever:	the most popular novel by Lever (1806–72) was *Charles O'Malley* (1840)
Charles Dickens:	Dickens (1812–72) excelled in presenting the life of nineteenth-century London, especially the life of the poor, in his famous novels. He edited the journal *Household Words*, 1850–59
make short work of it:	finish it off quickly
Tauchnitz:	a German publishing firm which issued paper-covered reprints of British and American authors
affiliate me:	connect me with
a Norwegian author:	Ibsen
Harry Lorrequer:	Lever's first novel, published anonymously in 1836
Shavian *Anschauung*:	combination of an adjective based on the name Shaw with a German noun more commonly used by English writers in the compound form, *Weltanschauung*, 'view of the world' or 'philosophy'
Henri Beyle:	*alias* Stendhal (1783–1842), French author whose classic novel, *Le Rouge et le Noir* (*Scarlet and Black*) was published in 1830
Potts:	leading character of Lever's *A Day's Ride: A Life's Romance*
Pozzo di Borgo:	Count Andrea Pozzo di Borgo (1764–1842) opposed Napoleon and became Russian Ambassador in Paris and then (1835) in London
Alnaschar:	a character from *The Arabian Nights' Entertainment* translated into English by Sir Richard Burton in 1885–8
Don Quixote:	the foolish knightly hero of Spain's great satirical romance of the same title (1605) by Miguel de Cervantes (1547–1616)
Simon Tappertit:	a character in Dickens's novel *Barnaby Rudge* (1841)

Aristophanes:	(c.450–c.385 BC) was the principal comic dramatist of ancient Greece. Shaw may have *The Clouds* (423 BC) specifically in mind
Stevenson:	Robert Louis Stevenson (1850–94), the Scottish novelist and man of letters, is best known today for the adventure stories, *Treasure Island* (1883) and *Kidnapped* (1886), and the psychological horror story, *Dr Jekyll and Mr Hyde* (1886). Shaw may here be thinking of his *New Arabian Nights* (1882)
William Hogarth:	(1697–1764) a leading English painter and satirical artist
Bedlam:	the Hospital of St Mary of Bethlehem in London, used as an asylum for the insane; from this the meaning of 'bedlam' was extended to refer to any insane asylum and, eventually, to denote a state of noise and chaos
Pistol:	a character in Shakespeare's *Henry IV, Part 2, Henry V* and *The Merry Wives of Windsor*; one of Prince Hal's low-life associates and a boastful comic idiot
Parolles:	a foolish character in Shakespeare's *All's Well That Ends Well*
Pickwick:	one of Dickens's best loved comic characters, the principal figure in *Pickwick Papers* (1837)
infatuate:	foolish; the adjective is rarely used
address:	preparedness, adroitness
pain in the self-esteem:	Shaw writes of self-love as a permanent part of the human organism which could be hurt like a leg or elbow
splenetic:	bad-tempered
A sentence... quoted:	Schopenhauer derided feminine physique as 'undersized, narrow-shouldered, broad-hipped and short-legged' in his essay 'On Women' (1851). He was equally uncomplimentary to the mental and moral character of women
Ernest Belfort Bax:	Bax (1854–1926) did not publish his main anti-feminist works until after *Major Barbara* appeared. These were: *The Legal Subjection of Men* (1908) and *The Fraud of Feminism* (1913). His *Essays in Socialism* was published in 1906
homoist:	advocating the rights and virtues of the male sex; the word is an invention on the model of 'feminist'
'soul... in things evil':	quoted from Shakespeare's *Henry V*, Act IV, scene i

mercanto-Christian: by inventing this compound term, Shaw manages to imply that commercialism (mercantilism) is part of the religion of modern Western civilisation

Jenseits von Gut und Böse: later translated and published as *Beyond Good and Evil* (1886)

'big blond beast': a phrase from Nietzsche's *Genealogy of Morals* (1887)

Superman ... borrowed by me: especially in the play *Man and Superman* (1901–3)

Captain Wilson: Frederick J. Wilson (dates uncertain) edited and largely wrote three numbers of *The Little Journal of New Ideas*, published by the Comprehensionist Association, from which he extracted a pamphlet, *The House that Jack Built* (1889). He mounted an exhibition, 'The Gallery of Ideas', in London, and published a catalogue to accompany it. His works follow in the ancient tradition of emblems and allegories, and his moralisation of the Citadel of Peace in the city of Willingwell may have suggested the town of Perivale St Andrews (an allegorical city as well as a mundane model town) in *Major Barbara*. Wilson uses the term 'Crosstianity' in an article entitled 'Cardinal Newman on Scriptural Inspiration and Principal Fairbairn on the Churches and the Ideal of Religion', in *The House that Jack Built*

the Dialectical Society: one of the socially progressive debating societies which flourished in London, and which Shaw used to attend

the beatitudes of the Sermon on the Mount: given in the Gospel of St Matthew, 5. The beatitudes most relevant to *Major Barbara* are: 'Blessed are the poor in spirit' and 'Blessed are the peacemakers'

Stuart-Glennie: John Stuart Stuart-Glennie (dates uncertain), author of *Pilgrim Memories* (1875)

Buckle: Henry Thomas Buckle (1821–62), British historian and pioneer of social history, influenced radical thinkers in many countries

a fantastic sally: an outburst of fanciful thinking

parthenogenetically: an exaggerated way of saying 'unaided', parthenogenesis being procreation without sexual union

cosmogonies: Shaw probably means 'theories of the universe and the laws governing it' ('cosmologies' would be the usual word)

The Gospel of St Andrew Undershaft

This discusses a principal theme of *Major Barbara*: poverty as an offence against true social morality and as a cause of other social evils. The false morality of contemporary society is attacked, including the hypocrisy of teaching disdain for money.

NOTES AND GLOSSARY:

St Andrew Undershaft: Undershaft in the play is not a saint, but refers to his beliefs as his 'gospel'; Shaw took the name from a church dedicated to St Andrew. See p. 21
to wit: specifically, to be precise; archaic expression
clearness of wit: Shaw is using 'wit' in the old sense of 'mind'
inoculation with smallpox: Shaw was a fierce opponent of compulsory inoculation and here refers to a contemporary medical theory that inoculation with the germ of one disease could cure another disease
torture in the solitary cell: imprisonment itself is the torture Shaw has in mind
the fine arts: especially music, painting, sculpture, literature, as distinct from the useful arts, or crafts
rickety: suffering from the disease of rickets, or rachitis, found in conditions of near-starvation
Let him be cheap: reference to the vicious practice whereby the unemployed were offered jobs at less than the basic rate of pay, as a pretext for reducing the wages of other workers
congeries: a collection of things heaped together; rarely heard today
the undeserving: Alfred Doolittle in Shaw's *Pygmalion* is an amusing spokesman for the class which late-Victorian sociologists labelled 'the undeserving poor'
lay up ... in heaven: an adaptation of the Biblical text, 'Lay not up for yourselves treasures upon earth, where moth and rust doth corrupt, and where thieves break through and steal: But lay up for yourselves treasures in heaven' (St Matthew 6:19–20)
hell upon earth: Shaw did not believe in any divinely decreed place of everlasting torment for the souls of the dead, but adapted the theological notion of hell to describe the evil conditions men create on this earth
every adult ... painlessly killed: it is important to remember that Shaw was writing to shock people, in the tradition of satirists such as Jonathan Swift (1667–1745) whose *Modest Proposal* for solving the problem of poverty in Ireland was that babies should be killed and eaten

Summaries · 53

radicle: tiny root
Cobden-Sanderson: Thomas James Cobden-Sanderson (1840–1922) founded the Doves Press which set superior standards in design and craftsmanship
Universal Pensions for Life: the idea Shaw attributes to Cobden-Sanderson became the basis of the Report of the Beveridge Commission, following the second world war, which introduced the so-called 'Welfare State' in Britain, through its plan for comprehensive social security for all citizens 'from the cradle to the grave'
'a reserve army of unemployed': three trade depressions in the last quarter of the nineteenth century had kept unemployment in the forefront of British public consciousness
the Kantian test: Immanuel Kant (1724–1804), leading German idealist philosopher, author of *The Critique of Pure Reason* (1781), expounded his famous doctrine of the categorical imperative in *A Metaphysic of Morals* (1785). He claimed that the moral virtue of a line of conduct should be judged according to what would result if it were made a general law for mankind
Lazarus... Dives: See p. 20 above. Dives is the rich man
Froissart's medieval hero: Jean Froissart (*c*.1333–*c*.1404), the French poet and historian, wrote a celebrated chronicle of French and English history from 1307 to 1400, a principal source of information on the Hundred Years' War between the two countries
pill: to plunder, to pillage; an old word
mouth-honor: the more usual expression is 'lip-service'
Ruskin: John Ruskin (1819–1900), a wealthy and very influential Victorian writer on art who became a radical social reformer and economist
William Morris: the pre-Raphaelite author and decorative artist, founder of the Arts and Crafts Movement, who lectured on socialism, edited the extreme socialist journal *Commonweal*, and spent a large part of his fortune in the socialist cause. See also pp. 7 and 43 above
Kropotkin: Prince Peter Kropotkin (1842–1921), a respected anarchist writer and social philosopher, lived in England from 1886 to 1917
bediamonded: covered with diamonds
Trade patterns: designs produced for commercial purposes

'slaughtered': late nineteenth-century slang usage applied to cabinet-makers as 'sweated' was to other overworked and under-paid craftsmen

the cash nexus: this famous phrase, summing up the theory that monetary relations form the only bond uniting capitalist society, is derived from Thomas Carlyle (1795–1881)

damned wantlessness: this phrase originated with Ferdinand Lassalle (1825–64), founder of the German Social Democratic movement

the esthetic life: this phrase had a very particular meaning in the context of the Aesthetic Movement of the late nineteenth century, which turned away from the ugliness of the industry and commerce on which British imperial prosperity was based, in search of an untainted beauty

the Kelmscott Chaucer: William Morris produced a beautiful hand-printed and decorated edition of Geoffrey Chaucer's (c.1345–1400) *Canterbury Tales* at his Kelmscott Press in 1896

cranks: eccentrics; the word was introduced into Britain from America in the late nineteenth century

Drury Lane pantomime: an annual Christmas pantomime at the Theatre Royal, Drury Lane, was popular family entertainment for Londoners throughout most of the nineteenth century and into the twentieth

temperance: at this period, the Temperance Movement aimed at improving the social condition of the poor by discouraging the drinking of alcohol

redemption ... erring brothers: Shaw here borrows the language of evangelical Christianity

the Trinity: the Father, the Son and the Holy Spirit of Christian belief; in an essay 'On Going to Church' (1896), Shaw gives his personal, humanist and anti-patriarchal alternatives: 'or Mother, Daughter ...'

demagogy: used here in the bad sense of political agitation

scapegoats: the term has lost most of its force through familiarity; it derives from a ritual of atonement laid down by the prophet Moses, whereby one of two goats was driven out into the wilderness, symbolically laden with the sins of the people, and the other was sacrificed

Will or Life Force: as in the play itself, Shaw uses 'Will' to suggest a relationship between the Christian notion of the

Summaries · 55

       Will of God and the Schopenhauerian concept of impersonal Will; 'Life Force', with which he equates it, is a key term in Shaw's philosophy, translating the phrase *élan vital* used by the French philosopher Henri Bergson (1859-1941)

artificial Darwinian darkness: Shaw accepted the theory of creative evolution derived from the French biologist Lamarck (1744-1829) and conveyed to him through Samuel Butler (see below); for him, this was a valid scientific alternative to Charles Darwin's (1809-82) theory of a struggle for the survival of the fittest in nature and the social conclusions drawn from it by those in favour of capitalist competition

the Euripidean republican: 'republican' may relate to the passage in Act III where Cusins identifies the temptation Undershaft offers with an idea expressed in Plato's *Republic*. See p. 46

per saltum: at a jump, in a single operation; Shaw removed this Latin phrase when he revised the Preface for publication with the screen version of *Major Barbara*

Samuel Butler: a satirist (1835-1902), the author of *Erewhon* (1872) and the autobiographical novel *The Way of All Flesh* (1903). Butler's arguments for creative evolution were presented in *Life and Habit* (1877) and *Evolution Old and New* (1886)

Laodiceanism: lukewarmness, apathy, the fault attributed to the church in Laodicea in the biblical Book of Revelations, 3:14-16

Alfred de Musset: (1810-57) a French poet and dramatist

Georges Sand: (1804-76) the pen name of a distinguished French woman novelist

author of Hudibras: another Samuel Butler (1612-80)

The Salvation Army
Shaw answers the charge that his play attacks the Salvation Army. He argues that his critics do not grasp, as religious organisations do, that every individual is implicated in his society and it is impracticable to distinguish ill-gotten money from other money.

NOTES AND GLOSSARY:
the despairing ejaculation... blasphemy: see note on 'My God... forsaken me', p. 38
Sir Oliver Lodge: (1851-1940) a distinguished physicist and pioneer in psychical research

Dr Stanton Coit: (1857–1944) a well-known minister of the Ethical Church in London

William Stead: W. T. Stead (1849–1912) was editor of the *Pall Mall Gazette* and founded *The Review of Reviews*

with vine leaves in his hair: the worshippers of Bacchus (or Dionysos) as god of wine are portrayed thus in art

religious character of the drama: late nineteenth-century and early twentieth-century scholars were united in the view that drama originated in religious ritual, whether ancient Greek or medieval Christian

where two or three: an allusion to Christ's words, 'where two or three are gathered together in my name, there am I in the midst of them' (St Matthew 18:20). Shaw's application of the phrase illustrates his humanist faith

mimes and mummers: somewhat literary terms for popular entertainers

teetotalism: the principle of abstinence from alcoholic drink

boys' brigade: 'an organisation of the boys connected with a church or mission, for purposes of drill and instruction' (Oxford English Dictionary)

a Chicago meat King: *The Jungle* (1906) by Upton Sinclair (1878–1968) exposed the exploitation of labour in the Chicago canned-meat industry. Shaw refers to this American novelist later

Mrs Warren's profession: prostitution; an allusion to Shaw's play of that name

the Pharisees: see note above, p. 21

Tom Hood shirts: Thomas Hood (1799–1845) wrote 'The Song of the Shirt' about the sweated home-labour of sewing women in the cotton industry

Barbara's Return to the Colors

Shaw makes the point that his heroine's disillusionment is not the end of the story, but a stage in her progress. He discusses the significance of the founder's choice of a military style of organisation and military symbolism for the Salvation Army.

NOTES AND GLOSSARY:

the colors: the banner of a regiment

General Booth: see note on the Salvation Army, p. 19

Blood and Fire: the motto combines the metaphor of a church militant with the traditional symbolism of blood and fire as cleansing, redemptive agents

hard words ... break no bones: adaptation of traditional rhyme, 'Sticks and stones may break my bones,/But hard words never hurt me'

Voltaire: François-Marie Arouet, called Voltaire (1694–1778), the great French satirist and rationalist

Rousseau: Jean-Jacques Rousseau (1712–78), a highly influential French author, whose works, based on an idealisation of the Natural Man, are generally regarded as initiating the Romantic Movement. As a political theorist he prepared the climate of thought for the French Revolution

the Encyclopedists: Diderot (1713–84), d'Alembert (1717–83) and their associates whose work on the French *Encyclopédie ou dictionnaire raisonné des sciences, des arts et des métiers* (28 volumes, 1751–65) was one of the greatest achievements of the Age of Enlightenment and helped to spread revolutionary views

the Social Contract: a notion developed in the seventeenth century by opponents of the theory of the divine right of kings, namely that government depends on a contract, open or tacit, agreed upon by the citizens. This theory was taken up by Rousseau who made it the title of a book of 1768 advocating democracy

September massacres: there were about twelve hundred victims of the revolution in Paris, after the collapse of the monarchy, in September 1792

Utilitarians: a British school of thinkers of the later eighteenth century and the nineteenth century whose philosophy was the basis of a political radicalism that prepared the way for socialism

Christian Socialists: a late-nineteenth-century group in England whose leaders included the novelist Charles Kingsley (1819–75). They believed that the Church should engage in the politics of social reform

Fabians: the Fabian Society was founded in 1884 and took its name from the legendary Roman, Fabius Cunctator, who waited until the time was ripe before he struck. Shaw joined the Society in its second year. It still exists

Bentham: Jeremy Bentham (1748–1832), philosopher of Utilitarianism (concerned with 'the greatest happiness of the greatest number') and leader of the Philosophical Radicals

Mill: John Stuart Mill (1806–73), the author of *Utilitarianism* (1861) and a classic essay *On Liberty* (1859), was Bentham's chief follower, an ardent social reformer and champion of women's rights

58 · Summaries

Carlyle:	Thomas Carlyle (1795–1881), the major nineteenth-century historian and prose writer, took on the function of prophet to Victorian England, attacking capitalism and the growth of democracy alike
Henry George:	(1839–97) an American economist, author of *Progress and Poverty* (1879)
More:	Sir Thomas More (1478–1535), Renaissance scholar, author of *Utopia*, and an eminent statesman, executed for his opposition to King Henry VIII's rejection of papal authority over the English Church
Montaigne:	Michel de Montaigne (1533–92), a famous French essayist
Molière:	Jean-Baptiste Poquelin, called Molière (1622–73), France's greatest writer of comic drama
Beaumarchais:	Pierre-Augustin de Beaumarchais (1732–99), a French playwright, author of *The Barber of Seville* (1775) and *The Marriage of Figaro* (1784). Beaumarchais' work was regarded as socially subversive
Goethe:	Johann Wolfgang von Goethe (1749–1832), the author of *Faust* and Germany's greatest writer, was also a scientist
Dickens' doctor in the debtor's prison:	in Chapter 6 of Dickens's novel *Little Dorrit* (1857)
duns:	debt collectors
the depressing noise called 'sacred music':	Shaw as a music critic was familiar with a type of music performed at 'sacred concerts': it was turned out by dull composers to meet the demands of a pious public that had little true appreciation of music

Weaknesses of the Salvation Army
After pointing out the weaknesses of the Army's tendency to bureaucracy and its financial dependence on the rich, Shaw criticises, as a non-Christian, the organisation's attachment to out-dated theology and excessive emphasis on eternal life. He considers that these dogmas are far removed from the values implied in the Salvationists' day-to-day work. He states his opposition to confession and absolution of sins, and argues instead for the acceptance of responsibility and the principle that conduct improves when individuals are respected and treated well within society. His argument favours basing political institutions on the idea of social equality – and democracy on moral toleration. The section ends with a warning of the dangers of terrorism which may arise out of the cynicism of the poor who come to recognise that charitable

organisations have to pay a high price to the State for survival and may become instruments for enforcing its rule.

NOTES AND GLOSSARY:

St William Booth: General Booth was never given the title of saint officially

Evangelicals: closely associated with Methodism and the Low Church element in the Church of England; pious folk, insistent on the Bible as the sole authority, hence narrow-minded

Commissioner Howard: T. Henry Howard (1849–1923) became Chief of Staff in the Salvation Army in 1912

Genesis ... species: Charles Darwin's *Origin of Species* (1859) outraged many orthodox Christians because its theory of evolution challenged the biblical account of Creation in the Book of Genesis

Jephthah: his story, told in the biblical Book of Judges, chapter 11, is memorable for the episode of his bargain with God that, in return for victory over his enemies, he would sacrifice whatever creature first came out to greet him on his return; this proved to be his daughter

Dagon or Chemosh: pagan gods (worshipped by the Philistines and Moabites respectively)

Frederick's grenadier: apparently an allusion to Frederick the Great of Prussia (1712–86) who spurred on his reluctant guards with the words, 'You rogues, do you want to live forever?'

the very diagnostic: the sure sign

scot and lot: this phrase originally denoted a tax levied to meet municipal expenses, but came to be used idiomatically, as here, in the sense of 'thoroughly'

battalions of the future: Shaw is extending the military metaphor

district visitors: a category of social workers

the salvation of the world by the gibbet: most Christians think of the Cross only as the symbol of their faith. Shaw counts on shocking them with a reminder of the original function of the cross in the execution of criminals

Crosstianity: the equivalent psycho-analytic term is 'sado-masochism'; see note on Captain Wilson, p. 51

poetic justice: ideal justice such as an imaginative author is able to deal out to his characters

Victor Hugo: (1802–85) a leading French Romantic poet, dramatist and novelist. The book referred to here is *Les Misérables* (1862)

buccaneers of the Spanish Main: pirates who sailed in the Caribbean sea; the phrase has a literary ring

Captain Kidd: William Kidd (c. 1645–1701), Scottish sailor who turned pirate and was ultimately hanged

marooned: put ashore on a desert island as a punishment

Trust magnate: wealthy man who is a dominant figure in the controlling group of a commercial company

gentleman of fortune: pirate; an ironical slang phrase favoured in the literature of romantic adventure

the torture house: Shaw's challenging euphemism for prison

the odor of sanctity: originally referred to the sweet smell reported to rise from the bodies of saints; commonly used sarcastically of a (perhaps false) reputation for virtue

the judicial bench: all the judges who preside over the courts of law

the episcopal bench: the congregation of all the bishops in the Church of England

the Privy Council: special advisers to the king or queen

the Old Bailey dock: the enclosed place occupied by prisoners on trial in the central criminal courts at the Old Bailey in London

suburban season ticket holder: an insignificant individual, one of the anonymous population of London, living in the suburbs and working in the centre

bounders: fashionable Edwardian slang term of abuse applied to untrustworthy, ill-behaved persons

caste: this word, as distinct from 'class', emphasises differences of birth rather than of wealth

Napoleon: Napoleon Bonaparte (1769–1821) created a new nobility in Europe when he became Emperor after leading the forces of the French Revolution

Julius Caesar: the appointment of Rufio by Caesar (?102–44BC) was dramatised by Shaw in *Caesar and Cleopatra* (1898)

Louis XI: (1423–83) became king of France in 1461, and proceeded to recruit members of the middle class as advisers to enable him to impose his authority on the great princes in his kingdom

Reigns of the Saints ... licentious Restorations: the outstanding example of such extremes in English history occurred when the Restoration of the monarchy with the accession of King Charles II (1660) ushered in a period of licentious reaction against the puritanism of the Commonwealth (1649–60). Several puritan sects designated themselves 'Saints'

a Russian man of genius: Maxim Gorky (1868–1936), novelist and dramatist

Tetzel: Johann Tetzel (c.1465–1519) was a successful preacher and seller of indulgences, in opposition to whom Martin Luther put forward his theses at Wittenberg in October 1517, inaugurating the Protestant break-away from the Catholic Church

sell absolution: Protestants regarded the habit of accepting money for forgiveness of sins as one of the great abuses of the Roman Catholic Church

conscience-money: unsolicited payments especially those made to the Inland Revenue (tax authorities), that ease the giver's conscience

chewing the cud of their reflections: a tautological expression, as the common metaphorical sense of 'chew the cud' is 'reflect, meditate'

every man has his price: probably the best known version of this proverb is attributed to Sir Robert Walpole (1676–1745), Prime Minister and founder of the Cabinet system. His use of the words was entirely cynical, as Shaw's is not

their sweaters: those who exploit their labour for profit

are rent: (*an archaism*) are torn

the one now in progress in Russia: a reference to the various revolutionary disturbances and political reforms of 1905 and 1906

the thirtysix articles . . . three more: those entering the priesthood of the Church of England have had to agree to 'the Thirty-Nine Articles' (statements of faith) since the list was drawn up in 1562

almoners of the rich: givers of charitable benefactions to the poor on behalf of the rich

Christianity and anarchism

Shaw gives an example of the unjust power of the State provoking individual violence: anarchist bomb-throwing at a royal wedding in Madrid. He contrasts two aspects of Christianity shown in reactions to this event: the one obsessed by the notion of punishment; and the other affirming equality and rejecting the cruelty and senselessness of penal measures.

NOTES AND GLOSSARY:

royal marriage: that of Princess Victoria Eugenia of Battenberg to King Alfonso XIII of Spain (1886–1941) which took place on 31 May 1906

chips ... veneering: damages the polished surface to show the (inferior) material beneath; a loose use of metaphor

crowned by plutocracy: the phrase implies that the monarchy was the tool of the wealthy

sixpennorth of fulminate: 'fulminate' is an acid-based explosive; the colloquial 'sixpennorth' ('six-penny-worth') suggests the amateurish nature of the explosive device used

Herod: reference to the slaying of all the male children of the Bethlehem region by Herod, King of the Jews, who had heard the prophecy of Christ's birth and feared him as a threat to his own power (see St Matthew 2)

'the whiff of grapeshot': a phrase used by Carlyle in *The French Revolution* (1834–7), Part I, Book 5, chapter 3

one of our dukes: John Campbell, ninth Duke of Argyll, Governor-General of Canada (1878–83), who died in 1914

would fain: would have preferred to; archaic expression

proletarians of the ducal kidney: a paradoxical phrase, implying that the working class reflects the aristocracy in supporting the use of violence against class enemies. The term for the organ of the body, 'kidney', is used to denote 'temperament', or 'kind', 'sort'

argute: this fairly unusual word means 'keen' or 'shrewd'; it is employed sarcastically here

Bobrikoff: the Russian Governor of Finland, General N. I. Bobrikoff (1839–1904), had recently been assassinated

De Plehve: a reactionary Russian statesman (1846–1904), recently assassinated

Grand Duke Sergius: a member of the Russian royal family (1857–1905), also assassinated

No : fulminate ... revolutionaries: the original meaning of the verb 'fulminate' is 'to thunder and lighten'; its common use today is in the sense of 'denounce or protest vehemently', but it apparently means 'blow up' here

English princess: the bride was Queen Victoria's grand-daughter, popularly known as Princess Ena

Ravaillac: François Ravaillac (1578–1610) assassinated King Henry IV of France

Damiens: Robert Damiens (1715–57), a fanatic who tried to assassinate King Louis XV of France, and, like Ravaillac, was terribly tortured before being put to death

grandee: a Spanish or Portuguese nobleman of highest rank, here used in recognition of moral worth. The reference is to José Nikens, editor of the radical newspaper, *El Motin*

the only editor in England..: George William Foote (1850–1915), who founded *The Freethinker* in 1881

Some conclusions

This section is concerned with the relative nature of morality and law and the fact that major social changes must be accompanied by a revision of official morality, or else individuals are driven into a war of conscience against society. Shaw proposes two necessary reforms for the 'salvation' of imperial Britain: the abolition of a leisure class that consumes without producing; and abolition of the prison system. He brings his commentary back to the characters of Barbara and Bill Walker, and remarks on the value of an awakened conscience as a preventative of crime. Finally, he distinguishes between religions that are not intellectually honest and fictions, like this play, which *are*.

NOTES AND GLOSSARY:

the Ribbon lodges of Ireland: the Ribbon Association was a Roman Catholic secret society started in Northern Ireland in the early nineteenth century. Like its Protestant enemy, the Orange Order, the organisation is divided into lodges

in the preamble or in the penalty: specialised legal usage denoting the opening section of a statute or formal document (preamble), and the final section stating the legal consequences of infringement

obsolescing: going out of date, decaying; the verb is rare

'What's Property? Theft!': quoted from Pierre-Joseph Proudhon (1809–65)

raising our gorge against: disgusting us with

empiricism in conduct: 'the doctrine which regards experience as the only form of knowledge'; Shaw seems to be using the phrase pejoratively, meaning 'conduct based on no principles at all'

vivisection: Shaw was well known for his strong opposition to scientific experimentation on living animals

economically disposed... old-maidishness: a variant on Shaw's previous description of himself as 'a hater of waste'. The timid old maid was a figure of popular imagination. In applying the image to himself, Shaw anticipated some of his critics

Manchuria: a reference to the Russo-Japanese war of 1904–5
the millennium: heaven on earth
soul atrophy disguised as empire: the thesis argued by Edward Gibbon (1737–94) in *The Decline and Fall of the Roman Empire* (1776–88)
if a dog delights: Shaw has adapted a line from Isaac Watts (1674–1748), a famous writer of hymns: 'Let dogs delight to bark and bite,/For God hath made them so'
it goes to the lethal chamber: legalistic way of saying 'it is put to death'
a manufactured penalty: an artificially devised punishment, as distinct from a natural consequence of misdeeds
systems of conscience banking: ways of amassing credit for socially beneficent actions
hospital subscription lists: lists of benefactors whose donations helped maintain hospitals
sacrificial lamb: traditional religious sacrifice, used as a symbol of Christ
deify human saviours ... virgin intercessors: Shaw extends the original Christian reference to Christ and the Virgin Mary to cover a modern social analogy: attributing special virtues to, and relying unduly upon, particular men and women (a way of evading personal responsibility)
attribute mercy to the inexorable: a reference to the theological notion of the crucifixion of Christ as winning the mercy of an angry God for the sins of men
hocus-pocus: fraudulent magic
the doom of Cain: the son of Adam and Eve, he slew his brother Abel (according to the Book of Genesis) and was condemned by God to be a wanderer and exile, branded as a warning to all men not to kill him. Shaw interprets the doom as consisting in living with the memory of a deed that cannot be expiated
according to Scripture: in the plain terms associated with the Bible. Shaw ends his prefatory essay with a parody of a ritual curse

Part 3

Commentary

The general nature of the play

Major Barbara is a play of ideas, one of Shaw's most successful attempts to deal with large subjects in a witty and entertaining fashion. Although it is set in England early in the twentieth century and its theatrical style is highly artificial, it is not difficult to translate the matters it is concerned with into terms equally challenging to us today. The problems of societies divided into rich and poor face us today on a world-wide scale. Undershaft's assertion, 'The more destructive war becomes, the more fascinating we find it', is more chilling and frightening in the late twentieth century than it was in 1905. Undershaft rejoices at the news of an aerial battleship which has proved itself by wiping out 'a fort with three hundred soldiers in it'; today he would be showing off his stockpile of nuclear bombs; he would offer Cusins a directorate in the firm on condition that he would pledge himself to sell missiles to any country, or revolutionary organisation, or private army, prepared to pay for them. For *Major Barbara* is a philosophical play, concerned with general principles which Shaw has illustrated here by using particular cases, inviting us to think about the nature of the world we live in, and the laws of human nature; about reality (which is the Undershaft inheritance in all its aspects).

Major Barbara is a dangerous play, best approached with caution and respect, not with the rashness of Charles Lomax throwing down a red-hot match in the shed where explosives are made. Shaw has deliberately formulated some of the ideas in the play in a striking and concentrated style that gives them great – and dangerous – force. Cusins's remark, 'The ballot paper that really governs is the paper that has a bullet wrapped up in it' must be a metaphorical statement, coming from such a character. But the line of thinking it represents challenges the traditional British belief in democracy, or government by consent, and leads logically to fascism, or government imposed by force and continually vulnerable to violent overthrow.

Use of actual letter-bombs is one of the consequences of accepting the idea. Few of us are safe among ideas: if we open our minds to one, we are only too liable to shut them again, as though that one idea was the whole truth. Barbara Undershaft's detestation of the great gap between the wealthy and the very poor has led her to dismiss her maid and try to live more simply; she has overlooked the damage done to the girl who lost her job. In studying the play we have to beware of extracting one idea or another, isolating particular passages from the total context, and assuming that we have mastered everything Shaw has to say. A good deal of the criticism of the play is based on just this mistake, underestimating the complexity and comprehensiveness of the dramatic structure.

This is not a propaganda play, preaching a single simple message in a narrowly doctrinaire way. It is less dangerous to treat it as a rag-bag of ideas which are tossed about for the fun of it without consistency or logic. Yet it is only possible to use it like that if we remain passive receivers, not attempting to grapple with the connections between ideas that the play makes; and productions which do not get involved – and involve their audiences – with the arguments in the play miss the sinewy quality, the urgency and cerebral excitement implicit in Shaw's text. *Major Barbara* is a training-ground for thinking; and we cannot appreciate it adequately unless we are prepared to exercise our minds to meet it, to think along the lines it proposes as though our lives depended upon it – as perhaps they do.

The intellectual elements in the play are not all abstract, verbally presented arguments. The story, the dramatic action, the characters – and the emotions they register and communicate – all feed our understanding.

Main themes

The legend of Saint Barbara

The story told dramatically in *Major Barbara*, in a short series of clearly defined incidents, has the power to affect us in various ways as a result of the different elements Shaw has brought together and the correspondences he suggests. His heroine shares her name with the patron saint of gunners and miners. According to the medieval Latin collection of pious stories, *The Golden Legend*, Barbara was the daughter of a wealthy pagan called Dioscurus who shut her up in a tower to protect her from those who came to seek her hand in marriage. On finding that she had been converted to Christianity, her father denounced her to the governing authorities who tortured her to make her renounce her faith. She remained firm, and Dioscurus was ordered to kill her. When he had done so, he was himself struck by lightning from heaven.

The special emblem associated with Saint Barbara is a tower, presented as a battlemented structure from which a cannon is directed, in a painting of Saint Barbara and her father by Peter Paul Rubens (1577–1640). This shows Barbara stepping up on to a stone platform beside the tower and turning to speak to Dioscurus who is obviously in enraged pursuit of her. There is a distinct similarity between this pictorial image and the setting of Barbara Undershaft's dispute with her father in the last scene of Shaw's play.

Shaw has used certain features of the saint's legend and left, or changed, others. The struggle between father and daughter over her faith is central to the play. The association with gunners and miners (who use dynamite) is transferred to the firm of Undershaft and Lazarus, and the lightning that kills is part of the potentially destructive elemental force that Undershaft represents as the source of all energy and power.

The life of Christ

According to orthodox doctrine, the lives of all the Christian saints reflect the story of Jesus Christ in some way. In fact, Shaw's story of Barbara Undershaft includes more parallels to the life of Christ than to the life of the saint. These can be indicated in summary form:

(a) the earthly family and heavenly origin of Jesus, incarnated as the child of a virgin mother	Barbara lives in her mother's house and does not know her father; every Undershaft is a foundling; Barbara and the Salvation Army know that she – and every human being – is a child of God, the Father in heaven
(b) the practical mission of feeding and healing	Barbara's work in the Salvation Army
(c) the temptation of Christ, symbolically presented in the Bible: the devil takes him up into a high place, shows him the kingdoms of this world and offers him power over them	Undershaft shows Barbara and the others round his ideal city of Perivale St Andrews, then takes her to the height overlooking the town, where he offers power over the town and its factories to Cusins and to Barbara
(d) Christ is sold into captivity by Judas, his disciple, for thirty pieces of silver	Undershaft succeeds in his plan to win Barbara by buying the Salvation Army with his cheque; this leaves her with the sense of having been betrayed, intensified when her lover goes off rejoicing with Undershaft and the Salvation Army band

(e) Christ dies a lonely and despairing death on the Cross	Barbara is left abandoned in the shelter, when she quotes the words of the dying Christ: 'My God: why hast thou forsaken me.' (Taking off her badge and, later, her uniform signifies the end of her old life)
(f) Christ descends into hell after death	Barbara goes to visit the munitions factory, expecting to find men like devils with blackened faces tending the flames; Undershaft insists on the evil – the slaying of innocent people – that brings joy to all there
(g) the Resurrection	Barbara's despair passes away, her faith is renewed and she starts a new life on the basis of a clearer understanding of reality
(h) the Ascension	Cusins comments on Barbara's new visionary enthusiasm: 'She has gone right up into the skies.'

Myth

One of the main characteristics of modernist literature (the experimental literature of the first half of this century) is its use of ancient myths (a) as an organising factor, giving unity to the work and often supplying the place of a newly invented plot; (b) to give depth and wide relevance to the work. Outstanding examples in English are: James Joyce's *Ulysses* (1922), T. S. Eliot's *The Waste Land* (1922), D. H. Lawrence's two-part novel *The Rainbow* (1915) and *Women in Love* (1922), the Cuchulain cycle of poems and plays by W. B. Yeats (published at intervals between 1904 and 1939), Eugene O'Neill's *Mourning Becomes Electra* (1931) – and G. B. Shaw's *Major Barbara* (1905) and *Heartbreak House* (1918). This literary phenomenon was a consequence of the decline of Christianity or acceptance of it as a purely symbolic system. It was allied to the growth of comparative religion and anthropology, as academic studies, and to the new science of psychoanalysis which drew on the universal stock of known myths to unlock the secrets of individual personality.

The outstanding nineteenth-century attempt to replace Christianity by another mythology was made by Richard Wagner (1813–83) in his cycle of music-dramas *The Ring of the Nibelungs*. In his prose works, Wagner declared his purpose of incorporating Christian and Greek values in a new system which would take form from Germanic tradition and aid the growth of the soul of the infant German nation. This was an instance of art taking over the function of religion in society. Wagner's achievement was ready-to-hand for use by the Nazi movement in our own century; it is a notable example of how dangerous art can be.

Shaw the music lover was an enthusiast for Wagner. Although his Preface attacks the assumption that the British have to borrow all their ideas from abroad, he was certainly acquainted with Nietzsche's essay, *The Birth of Tragedy from the Spirit of Music*, which was inspired by Wagner and re-interpreted ancient Greek culture, while attacking Christianity as a slave religion that over-valued suffering, humility and pity. Shaw's friend Gilbert Murray, the model for the character of Adolphus Cusins (see p.73), was one of a group of British classicists who studied Nietzsche with interest and promoted the understanding of ancient Greek drama in terms of its origin in religious beliefs and practices.

In following the lines of the life of Christ as narrated in the Bible for the construction of his story of Barbara Undershaft, Shaw was using the central Christian story as a myth: how much factual truth there is in it does not matter to his play; he can take it as a symbolic system and develop his own meanings from it. Like Wagner (and some of the writers referred to above), he has not confined himself to using the Christian myth. Perhaps encouraged by Gilbert Murray, he has combined elements from Greek mythology with it.

(a) The stories of Persephone and Eurydice
By choosing as his central character a young woman who is drawn away from her all-providing mother by 'the Prince of Darkness', Shaw removes his play a little from the Christ motif towards the legend of Persephone. Comparative mythologists classify this as a death-and-resurrection myth, similar to the myth of Christ's death and resurrection, but different in being specifically a nature myth. Persephone is the daughter of Demeter, the Earth goddess. While gathering flowers in the fields, Persephone is seen by Dis (Pluto is the Roman equivalent), the god of the underworld, who seizes her and carries her off to his kingdom of death. All creation mourns her loss, and wintry conditions replace the abundant harvests. Demeter appeals to Zeus, chief of the gods, and the story ends with a compromise: Persephone is restored to her mother and the light of the sun for half the year, but must spend the other half in the underworld. This myth is connected with the idea of the seed having to lie dormant in the earth during winter, if the crops are to appear again in spring. There are

similarities in the story of Orpheus (prototype of the poet) who wins the release of his wife Eurydice from the underworld by going there himself and using his musical and poetic art on Pluto (unlike Cusins, bargaining with Undershaft, he loses her again).

(*b*) *Dionysos and Apollo*
Dionysos is one of several names playfully used by Cusins in addressing Undershaft. It is the name of the Greek god of wine (equivalent of the Roman Bacchus), a fertility god associated with suffering, another deity who dies and is re-born. Dionysos was the inspirer of music and poetry; and the dramatic forms of tragedy and comedy are traditionally regarded as originating in ancient festivals celebrating his power. Apollo, the sun god, god of music and poetry and founder of the art of statuary, is usually portrayed as a young man. He is not named directly in Shaw's play, but Cusins himself, chanting his own version of Euripides's choruses, is the 'lyric Apollo' figure balancing Dionysos Undershaft. The re-birth theme emerges in the idea of the foundling who becomes Andrew Undershaft upon his predecessor's death.

However, the form of the mythic story of Dionysos that Shaw used in *Major Barbara* follows the lines of Nietzsche's analysis of the history of ancient Greek culture. The German scholar told how ecstatic religions from further east infiltrated Greek society, previously noted for rationality and moderation. There followed a struggle between the old values and the new forces which reached a point of tension expressed by Nietzsche in terms of a truce after warfare: 'the Delphic god (Apollo) was now contented to take the destructive armaments from the hands of his powerful antagonist (Dionysos)'. This he represented as the cultural situation which gave rise to the greatest achievements of ancient Greece – above all to the art of Greek tragedy – and was marked by 'festivals of world-redemption and days of transfiguration'.

Nietzsche admitted that he was arbitrarily applying the description 'dionysiac' to a range of qualities and values that Christianity tended to reject; he was narrating his own artificially constructed myth as a means of stating his argument more vividly. The method was successful in catching the attention of a wide public, and the term 'appollinian' became as commonly used to describe the qualities of reason, discipline, control and dispassionate calm as 'dionysiac' to describe wild emotion and the frightening power of what became increasingly known as 'the unconscious'.

Shaw brings together elements of Christian and Greek tradition when Cusins explains the Salvation Army to Undershaft as: 'the army of joy, of love, of courage' which 'reveals the true worship of Dionysos' to the Professor of Greek.

Popular elements

The inclusion of myth in modern fiction may lead to ponderousness and may tempt readers into tracking down allusions and hunting out parallels and neglecting other aspects of the work. Shaw has guarded against this risk by combining his use of myth with elements that frighten off pedants and attract unpretentious people ready to be entertained in quite simple ways. In his Preface to *Three Plays for Puritans* (1901) he declared:

> My stories are the old stories; my characters are the familiar harlequin and columbine, clown and pantaloon...; my stage tricks and suspenses and thrills and jests are the ones in vogue when I was a boy, by which time my grandfather was tired of them.

The Christmas pantomime, which whole families went to see, was a very popular form of theatrical entertainment in Britain at the end of the nineteenth century. Part of the charm of the pantomimes was that they offered variations on a few familiar plots, commonly drawn from fairy tales and well known to children. Whatever the particular story presented, all pantomimes had important features in common, including:

(i) a sham villain who ranted and roared without really frightening, and was often known as the Demon King
(ii) an actress dressed in man's clothes who played the young hero: the Principal Boy
(iii) a male actor disguised as a middle-aged woman, sometimes supposed to be the mother of the Principal Boy; this was the Pantomime Dame, a broadly comic figure of a type popular in the contemporary music halls frequented by lower-class adult audiences
(iv) one or more other comic figures of a clownish type.

It is not difficult to see Lady Britomart as a haughty upper-class version of the Pantomime Dame, and it is hard to believe that Undershaft is an evil character, though the flames of his furnaces are at his back and he boasts of the destructiveness of his weapons; to Cusins he appears 'a most infernal old rascal' who appeals greatly to his 'sense of ironic humour' – like a Demon King. The military title and uniform given to Barbara by the Salvation Army and the jolly temperament she shows in Act I and much of Act II recall the Principal Boy.

Charles Lomax is the obvious clown. He is good-natured but incredibly stupid. He frequently blunders, making social mistakes that would be embarrassing in actual life but arouse laughter in an audience or reader. His thoughtlessness is matched by his inarticulacy: his part in the dialogue is loaded with repetition of 'Oh I say', 'you know', or 'dont you know', interlaced with a tissue of slang phrases. P. G. Wodehouse (1881–1975), a popular and skilful writer of farcical stories, was to create a whole gallery of young men-about-town resembling Charles Lomax. Stephen Undershaft is another type of clown: taking himself with great seriousness, he becomes a source of amusement as bores in art may be, whereas in life they are merely tedious.

We can even list Adolphus Cusins among the clowns. He is as ready to join in the fun as Lomax is, and enjoys teasing Lady Britomart: a clever clown whose astuteness and wit connect him with the traditional Harlequin mentioned by Shaw in the quotation above. When Barbara is downcast, his mischievous gaiety is intensified – the spirit of tragedy is not in him – and his exuberant mood maintains the continuity of the comedy through into the last act where she recovers her optimism.

Shaw never despised farce, usually classified as a 'low' form of comedy that makes people laugh at physical mishaps, ridiculous stage tricks and silly incidents that will not bear rational analysis. Among the details of *Major Barbara* that are farcical in themselves, or suggest farce, may be listed:

Bill Walker's narrative of how Todger Fairmile dealt with him

Snobby Price, having just 'confessed' publicly how he used to beat up his mother, running away when she comes to find him

the millionaire playing the trombone and marching with the Salvation Army band

Cholly explaining to the munition-makers how safe it is to put a match to gun cotton.

Each of these incidents makes a point that is relevant to the play's central themes, but we do not have to think it out before we laugh. Laughter is the result of an instantaneous perception, swifter than thought and in some way pleasurable. The characters of Lady Britomart, Stephen and Charles Lomax are very different from each other in most ways, but they all provoke laughter almost continuously.

Another form of popular entertainment which Shaw draws upon is the folk tale: those stories told orally from generation to generation and found, with variations, all over the world. Features of the plot of *Major Barbara* which recall folk tales are:

the condition on which the Undershaft wealth may be inherited: it can only go to a foundling (which brings in the elements of luck and chance)

the young hero, (comparatively) poor and of humble birth, is accepted as heir to the most powerful man in the country (often the king) and wins the hand of his daughter in marriage.

Other folk tale themes embedded in the text include:

> the test set for Charles Lomax whereby anything he is able to earn through his own endeavours will be doubled
>
> the story of how Adolphus met and fell in love with Barbara, believing her to be a poor girl, only to discover later that she is an aristocrat from a wealthy and powerful family.

Other themes

The Professor of Greek

The play was an extension of friendship between two men who struck sparks off each other's minds; and this was one source of the liveliness and high spirits that mark its treatment of very serious topics. Shaw acknowledged as much in his dedication:

> My play stands indebted to Gilbert Murray in more ways than the way from Athens.

The wording of this keeps private between them more than it states to the public. Within the text of *Major Barbara* Cusins makes a joke about Cholly's expression, 'a bit thick' (Act I), which is literally as well as metaphorically impenetrable Greek to modern audiences. It was audacious of Shaw to include it: he was enjoying himself playing a kind of game in preparing the play. It was natural that elation at his theatrical success should spill over into the new work and energise it.

He and Gilbert Murray were both giving financial support to Granville Barker's management of the Court, as well as supplying plays for his programme. For Murray it was a holiday interlude after a period of ill-health due to overwork. An Australian by birth, he had been appointed Professor of Greek at Glasgow University when he was twenty-three, after a brilliant career at Oxford where he was made a Fellow of New College. While at Glasgow, he had published his *History of Ancient Greek Literature* (1897). He was an enthusiast for the modern theatre, too, and had had an impressive melodrama, *Carlyon Sahib*, produced in 1899. It was as fellow members of the Committee working to bring a British National Theatre into being that he and Granville Barker first met, and Barker directed four of Euripides's plays in verse adaptations by Murray, alongside eleven plays by Shaw, at the Court Theatre, 1904–1907. The first of these, *Hippolytus*, had been received by the audience with calls for the author, meaning Murray. So Undershaft's nickname of Euripides for Cusins would have been understood by regular attenders at Court Theatre plays. The fun was carried further by making up Granville Barker, who played Cusins, to look like Murray, while the actor who played Undershaft was made up to look like Shaw. Workers in the theatre had their own title for *Major Barbara*: *Murray's Mother-in-Law*, referring to Lady Britomart as a comic caricature of the Countess of Carlisle, whose daughter had become Lady Mary Murray.

One of the key passages in *Major Barbara* was inserted by Shaw at a late stage in his writing of the play:

> UNDERSHAFT: ... Remember the words of Plato.
> CUSINS: ... Plato! You dare quote Plato to me!
> UNDERSHAFT: Plato says, my friend, that society cannot be saved until either the Professors of Greek take to making gunpowder, or else the makers of gunpowder become Professors of Greek.

Undershaft's words are a free paraphrase of Plato's statement in *The Republic* that the ideal ruler must be a philosopher. The passage sounds like an echo of actual discussions between the dramatist and his scholar friend; it also anticipates Murray's later career. He was appointed Regius Professor of Greek at Oxford in 1908 and divided the rest of his long and distinguished career between classical scholarship and work for the prevention of future wars through the development of international government. He worked for the League of Nations at Geneva, for the Council for Education in World Citizenship and the League of Nations Union within Britain; and he became president of the Committee for Intellectual Co-operation between nations. In this way Murray honoured Cusins's pledge to 'make war on war'.

Andrew Undershaft's profession

This heading was at one time Shaw's idea for the title of his play. It would have matched the titles of his earlier works, *Cashel Byron's Profession* (a novel), and *Mrs Warren's Profession*. In each of the three, the author has taken some way of making money that is considered disgraceful by society generally, though it may not actually be illegal. He shows how it is part of a total social and economic fabric, and how everyone is implicated in it by reaping benefits from the system. Cashel Byron's profession is prize-fighting, which Shaw presents as an image of the competitive society, with its capitalist gambling. Mrs Warren's profession is prostitution, especially prostitution organised as big business, and Shaw draws parallels with the contemporary position of women in marriage and, more broadly, with the exploitation of workers by capitalist firms and their shareholders.

In choosing the manufacture of armaments to concentrate on this time, he had two actual personalities to consider, both much in the public eye. The first was Alfred Nobel (1833–96), the Swedish inventor of dynamite, who became a multi-millionaire industrialist and left a fortune for the establishment of annual prizes for outstanding achievements in different fields of endeavour anywhere in the world, including the Nobel prize for work in the cause of universal peace. (The first awards had been made as recently as 1901.) The other personality was Basil Zaharoff (1849-1936), an armaments magnate and international financier of enormous wealth and political influence. Popular newspapers built up an image of Zaharoff as a mysterious figure of uncertain origins, sinister, and undoubtedly capable of claiming with Undershaft: 'I am the government of your country'. The German firm of Krupp may have supplied the idea of a family in which the manufacture of armaments is a hereditary profession.

Garden cities

Undershaft as a model employer recalls two paternalistic capitalists: George Cadbury (1839-1922) and W. H. Lever (1851-1925) who had built model towns for their workers, calling them respectively Bourneville (for the Cadbury chocolate firm) and Port Sunlight (for workers in the Lever soap factory). The architects employed in these developments were influenced by William Morris's idealised notion of the medieval village, and the whole project had oblique links with socialist ideas. Shaw, as a London borough councillor, had attended a conference of the Garden City Association at Bourneville in 1901. The founder of this Association, Ebenezer Howard (1850-1928), thought of the Garden City as a form of commune, through which a de-centralised society might supersede capitalism non-violently, and his book *Tomorrow: a Peaceful Path to Real Reform* (published in 1898, re-issued as *Garden Cities of Tomorrow* in 1902) won the approval of many Liberals. Shaw was a supporter of the foundation in 1903 of Howard's first Garden City at Letchworth, near his home at Ayot St Lawrence, and equally close to the small town of Stevenage. (Lady Britomart's father is the Earl of Stevenage.)

Perivale St Andrews is more like the creations of Cadbury and Lever than the utopias of co-ownership and co-operation advocated by Howard. Edwardian audiences, familiar with current arguments for and against the Garden City movement, may have been readier than we are to judge the political significance of Undershaft's model town.

Mephistopheles and 'diabolonian ethics'

One of the names applied to Undershaft is Mephistopheles. It is the name of the devil in the Faust legend, the Renaissance transformation of the story of Christ's temptation by the devil into terms especially suited to a period of expanding knowledge and mastery of the material world.

In modern times (since Goethe) Mephistopheles has sometimes been presented as an agent in Faust's spiritual growth through the knowledge of good and evil. Shaw's Preface to *Three Plays for Puritans* refers to the century between William Blake (1757–1827) and his own play *The Devil's Disciple* as a period when old ideas of good and evil and old views of the devil were being inverted in serious literature. He mentions as one example 'Nietzsche and his Good and Evil Turned Inside Out', and calls the type of radical challenge to conventional morality that he has in mind 'diabolonian ethics', making it clear that he values a moral sense, alert and responsible in particular situations, far above pious adherence to a cut-and-dried system of conduct. Undershaft attacks the accepted religion and social morality associated with the Church of England. His message to Barbara and Cusins could be summed up in lines from Blake's long allegorical poem, *Jerusalem* (his Utopia or the Garden City):

I care not whether a Man is Good or Evil; all that I care
Is whether he is a Wise Man or a Fool. Go! put off Holiness,
And put on Intellect.

Yet it is not clear that the world will be a very different place, at the end of the play, when Barbara's old religion has been destroyed and replaced by a new understanding of reality. Lady Britomart seems perfectly content to take over Perivale St Andrews.

The play of thought

This kind of uncertainty, or ambiguousness, is characteristic of *Major Barbara* and is not to be dismissed as a sign of the author's confusion in thought or expression. 'Truth is rarely pure and never simple', wrote Oscar Wilde, and Shaw looks all round the questions under debate between the characters in *Major Barbara*, demonstrating the complexity of the truth about them, making us recognise the validity of opposed arguments. He uses a variety of techniques for the exploration and presentation of ideas, including:

(*a*) logically developed argument
(*b*) debate
(*c*) dialectics
(*d*) paradox
(*e*) aphorism
(*f*) metaphor
(*g*) symbolism
(*h*) irony

Much of the richness, liveliness and provocative quality of the play comes from the way these techniques are intermingled and varied. The natural exuberance of Shaw's mental processes is transformed into an art of thinking which can delight with its charm, elegance, agility, the kind of beauty we call wit.

Argument and debate

The whole development of the play, including Barbara's leaving of the Salvation Army and Cusins's decision to join Undershaft's firm, demonstrates:

(*a*) the close connection between money and power
(*b*) the impossibility of reforming society if this connection is ignored
(*c*) the inadequacy of late nineteenth-century Christianity as a moral base for those who want to govern or change society, however good their intentions may be.

Andrew Undershaft presents this argument verbally, and, in an important letter to Gilbert Murray about the play, Shaw stated: 'I am of the mind that Undershaft is in the right, and that Barbara and Adolphus, with a great deal of his natural insight and cleverness, are very young, very romantic, very academic, very ignorant of the world.' The exposition of the argument is made more lively, more urgent and pointed by the debate: the systematic questioning, the contradiction and qualification of Undershaft's views by Cusins, Barbara and, more spasmodically, by most of the other characters. His chief opponents remind us continually of the horrifying implications of some of the things Undershaft says.

The challenge to Christian beliefs and principles is reinforced by the subplot in which the aggressive Bill Walker – like Barbara in the main plot – is ultimately saved from Christianity.

Dialectics

Through the debate, Shaw encourages dialectical thinking: a mode of reasoning that takes into account contradictory views in order to reach a more comprehensive understanding. This means more than doing justice to other people's views when they are different from ours; it involves considering what objections might be raised to our views, even when others have not criticised them. Oscar Wilde summed up the basis of dialectics in a paradox: 'That only is a truth . . . whose opposite is also true'. This strikes at the root of Stephen's assertion, 'Right is right; and wrong is wrong', by insisting that the opposite of right need not be wrong, and indeed there is always some other truth to be grasped that we have not taken into account. Dialectics is thus a means of opening up the closed mind.

Undershaft's opposite truths continually challenge the others' beliefs. In particular, he advises Cusins that money and gunpowder, not 'Baptism and the Supper of the Lord', are the 'two things necessary to Salvation', arguing that poverty is a crime, not a virtue or misfortune, opposing the Christian doctrine that man's soul is in danger from the seven deadly sins of pride, lust, greed, anger, envy, avarice and sloth with his alternative list: 'Food, clothing, firing, rent, taxes, respectability and children'. He is not alone in offering a revised version of the Christian liturgy, the chief prayers and formulations of Christian belief, which emerges at intervals throughout the play; Cusins makes his contribution near the end of Act I by challenging the terms of the General Confession:

> You would have to say before all the servants that we have done things we ought not to have done... I cannot bear to hear you doing yourself such an injustice... As for myself, I flatly deny it: I have done my best;

and Barbara, in Act III, speaks a new version of the Lord's Prayer that challenges the traditional Christian words:

The Lord's Prayer	*Barbara's Version*
Give us this day our daily bread	I have done away with the bribe of bread
Thy will be done on earth as it is in heaven	Let God's work be done for its own sake... because it cannot be done except by living men and women
Forgive us our debts as we forgive our debtors	When I die, let him be in my debt, not I in his; and let me forgive him...

Paradox and aphorism

By the limited standards of logic, paradoxical statements are self-contradictory nonsense; but pondering them forces the mind beyond its habitual limits to perceive new truths. The device is often used to convey mystical illumination, beyond the reach of reason: the mythic notion of dying into life is a paradox which is implied in Barbara's spiritual recovery from loss of faith. The force of a paradox may be intensified by using the concentrated verbal form of aphorism, as in Undershaft's question, 'Dare you make war on war?' or his identification of his 'best friend' as 'My bravest enemy'. The paradoxical idea that selling the soul is necessary to salvation is expressed in a variety of ways in both the dialogue and some of the incidents in the play.

Not all the aphorisms in the dialogue are paradoxical. 'Whatever can blow men up can blow society up', 'Thou shalt starve ere I starve', are not paradoxes, but their artfully compressed wording gives them the impact of bullets. It also makes them memorable, so that we may recall and consider them when the play has ended. We may accept a line such as 'All have the right to fight: none have the right to judge' when Undershaft says it, only to realise later that it is an ambiguous and highly questionable statement.

Metaphor and symbolism

The name of the Salvation Army is a paradox in itself, in view of Christ's insistence on love as the cornerstone of his gospel. It was adopted as a metaphor representing spiritual struggle in terms of physical warfare. (Similarly, the body of active, confessed Christians is traditionally called the Church Militant.) Variations on this idea appear frequently as verbal metaphors in *Major Barbara* as when Andrew advises the young people to 'kill' poverty and slavery, or asserts that 'The ballot paper that really governs is the paper that has a bullet wrapped up in it'. The metaphor is also implied in incidents reported or enacted on stage: we hear that Todger Fairmile wrestled against his salvation harder than against his Japanese antagonist in the fight at the music hall (here we have a simile); his physical defeat of Bill Walker is a comic symbol of his spiritual triumph; the drum (which helps keep up an army's courage for battle) is a symbol of enthusiasm but, when Adolphus and Barbara kiss across it, the connotations of enmity and strife are included in a stage image, emblematic of a reconciliation of opposite values. The army metaphor is translated into the symbolic setting of the final scene: the fortress with dummies lying about like dead soldiers, which recalls traditional allegories of the soul besieged within its castle of the body. (By contrast, the library of Act I is an apt – though not allegorical – setting for untested liberal ideas and sentiments.)

Shaw's deliberate shifts between literal and metaphorical uses of his vocabulary of violence jolt us as Undershaft's listeners are jolted by the realisation that the troops killed by the aerial battleship are not dummy soldiers. There is a troubling ambiguousness in Cusins's description of the weapons he wants to make, 'simple enough for common men to use, yet strong enough to force the intellectual oligarchy to use its genius for the common good', and an apparent contradiction between his belief that 'all power is spiritual' and his respect for the material force that 'can destroy the higher powers just as a tiger can destroy a man'. The author is moving us towards an understanding that the dynamite factory is a symbolic powerhouse, uniting literal references and metaphysical meanings, and that the raw materials used there are the ultimate energies, that can change the world or destroy it. This involves seeing a unity beyond the distinction between physical and spiritual, in keeping with the understanding of reality Barbara reaches, when she sets aside the moralistic distinction between clear-cut categories of good and wicked.

Irony

Barbara clings to the thought that 'There must be some truth or other behind all this frightful irony'. Undershaft's role in the play is like that of Socrates in the dialogues of Plato: he teaches the others (and us, through the others) by questioning them and showing up the fallacies and inconsistencies in their thinking; he deliberately leads them into mental traps in order to convince them of their intellectual errors. He is continually edging them towards his own greater awareness. Like a very clever chess player, he can see the whole game in his mind, while the others rarely see beyond the next move. In this sense he is an ironist, concealing most of what is in his mind until the others discover it for themselves; or understanding the situation more fully than they do. Perhaps the sharpest illustration of this irony comes in his statement 'Genuine unselfishness is capable of anything', with which Barbara eagerly agrees. She is thinking only of the courage, effort, self-sacrifice that unselfish people can show in their care for others; but his statement also covers the unscrupulous behaviour, sins and crimes that people are capable of, when they care less for their own souls and reputations than for the welfare of those they love, or the cause they serve. Undershaft's comment includes the reflection that 'the end justifies the means' (a familiar aphorism not quoted in the play).

Cusins perceives this and registers his awareness by quietly addressing Andrew as 'Mephistopheles! Machiavelli!' As we would expect, Cusins is quicker than the others, all the time, in detecting what is in Undershaft's mind. He is being driven to admit what he already knows, and he soon sees the logic of the Undershaft philosophy. As he is so much ahead of Barbara in this realisation, and as his scholarly attachment to the truth is stronger than his wish to protect her from it, he too becomes an ironist and joins in complicity with Undershaft, watching Barbara without interfering. Yet he still finds repugnant the truth that the other enjoys presenting.

Making Undershaft look like Shaw, on the stage, suggests that the character's views may be identified with the author's; but irony has its secrets to keep, and it will not do to assume that Undershaft, or any other character, expresses Shaw's view in whole or in part, consistently through the play. The ironic method leaves the questions with us.

The settings and theatrical styles

One way in which Shaw's theatrical sense prompted him to keep his play lively is his use of three sharply contrasted backgrounds. Act I and the first scene of Act III take place in Lady Britomart's imposing and comfortable library. Act II and the second scene of Act III are set out-of-doors: the first in the cold and poverty-stricken surroundings of the shelter; the second by implication in more temperate weather (there is no sign of snow here, as there was in Act II, and the flowers Lady Britomart carries are reminders of spring or summer) at the sham fort constructed for the testing of weapons. This last is a kind of stage set in itself, not a realistic environment. It matches the more abstract style of drama, the philosophic debate which dominates the end of the play, and gives it more urgency by symbolically reminding us of what is at stake. It also emphasises the fact that the discussion is itself a kind of battle.

A more obvious contrast in dramatic styles goes with the contrasted settings of the first two acts. Act I is a comedy of manners, almost as absurd as Oscar Wilde's (1854–1900) *The Importance of Being Earnest* (1899), an extremely witty farce of high society, which had appeared just over ten years earlier and also has a plot concerned with a foundling and a domineering aristocrat, Lady Bracknell, less pleasant than Lady Britomart. Act II presents the other extreme of society in a group of low-class characters ranging from the respectable and virtuous Jenny Hill and Peter Shirley through the sly trickster, Snobby Price, to the self-assertive bully, Bill Walker. (It is a sign of Shaw's personal sensitivity to the constraints Edwardian society put on its drama that Rummy Mitchens is not straightforwardly presented as an aged prostitute.) Bill Walker resembles the villainous Bill Sykes in Charles Dickens's novel *Oliver Twist* (1837–39), whose murder of his girl Nancy is a famous and most powerfully described melodramatic incident.

The term 'melodrama' originated with a popular type of nineteenth-century play, tense thrillers in which, usually, an innocent woman was threatened by an evil man and was rescued by a brave young hero. The quality of melodrama enters Act II of *Major Barbara*, strengthened by the East End setting, a familiar background to many such squalid and violent stories; but it is interwoven with a comedy subtler and more ironic than we find in Act I; and part of the subtlety is that what Undershaft is doing, observed and even commented on by Cusins, passes unnoticed by Barbara until too late.

Shaw has taken no trouble to conceal the sources on which he has drawn; indeed it was normal practice for him to comment on life indirectly, in his novels and plays, through variations or parodies of other literary works. This separates him from the naturalists who try to make art as indistinguishable from life as they can.

Characterisation and the grouping of characters

Shaw is not a naturalistic playwright intent on persuading us that his characters are real people. In keeping with the philosophical nature of his play, he offers us human images that are also devices for presenting an argument in a dramatic and entertaining form. Yet they are vivid and distinctive and give actors the opportunity to dazzle audiences with their performances. Indeed it is instructive to note that the least developed characters, Mrs Baines or Sarah, seem most like ordinary human beings; we accept them as 'normal' because there is not much to notice about them. Otherwise Shaw has drawn on stock theatrical or literary types to give simplified impressions of different temperaments and kinds of social behaviour: Lady Britomart, the haughty dowager; Undershaft, the domineering captain of industry; Cholly, the 'silly ass'; Stephen, the humourless prig; Bill, the surly proletarian bully; Jenny Hill, in whom we recognise the virtuous and defenceless heroine of so many nineteenth-century melodramas. However, the types have been made more complex and enriched. The threads of myth in the play help create the illusion that Undershaft and Lady Britomart, especially, are larger than life, slightly parodic versions of gods such as the burlesque theatre of the nineteenth century sometimes presented. Barbara, seen as a female Christ or Persephone figure, is a less exaggerated idealisation, further modified by the mistakes of youthful inexperience which she makes. The allegorical tradition in which personified abstractions serve as characters, has contributed, too: Lady Britomart is almost a personification of aristocracy and possessiveness; Bill Walker personifies physical violence in opposition to Cusins's rationality. In the screen version, Undershaft states explicitly: 'There are mystical powers above and behind the three of us', thus inviting a view of himself grouped with Cusins and Barbara as a Trinity of power, intellect and love, replacing the Trinity of orthodox Christianity. (This iconography is not stable: Lady Britomart edges her way in, disturbing the pattern.) Any danger that the characters may be reduced to allegorical ciphers is counteracted by the introduction of humanising detail: Andrew's account of the days of his poverty, or Lady Britomart's pain on being rejected by Stephen.

Occasionally Shaw sacrifices consistency to some other effect. So the foolish Cholly is given some unconventional and penetrating ideas to express in his own slangy style (for instance, 'there is a certain amount of tosh about this business of wickedness. It doesn't work.'). In fact, it is a feature of Shaw's drama that practically every character is allowed to contribute his or her own share of truth.

He has endowed Cusins and Undershaft with his own capacity for thinking seriously and humorously at the same time. This brings them to life in the text and on the stage. To Barbara he has given the ordinary human qualities of friendliness, warmth and sincerity, together with his own diffused, rather impersonal benevolence towards all mankind and sense of purpose in serving the community. She is the emotional centre of the play, yet we probably watch her with sympathy, like Cusins, rather than empathising strongly with her; for Shaw has difficulty in expressing strong emotion, and the nearest he comes to writing a passionate speech for Barbara is in the rhetorical enthusiasm of the final scene, when it is the mythic, divine aspect of the character that speaks.

Stage conditions and style

Shaw wrote for the typical nineteenth-century theatre with a proscenium arch framing the stage, combined with footlights and a pit for the orchestra which separated actors from audience. This encouraged a rhetorical style of dialogue and mode of acting, concerned to make its points strongly, as an exciting public speaker does. It was a highly artificial style and has been scorned in the twentieth century for its exaggerations and generally superseded by other styles mostly formed in smaller theatres and aiming at a more natural effect. Harley Granville Barker (1877–1946) was among those responsible for the direction of the change (see p. 11) so it is not surprising that Shaw occasionally complained that Barker's way of producing them did not suit his plays, which he compared with Italian opera. The two men, working in collaboration, achieved a very effective balance. A well-known critic praised the acting at the Court Theatre as 'entirely natural and not calculated for effect', but one of the actors later commented on this: 'he testified that what was perhaps the most calculated and even stylised acting I have ever known succeeded in its effect'.

Part 4

Hints for study

THERE IS NO SINGLE RIGHT INTERPRETATION of any text; the better we get to know the work, the more we are likely to find in it. Yet misinterpretations are certainly possible and need to be avoided by attentive reading and re-reading to ensure that:

what the author has written is understood accurately;
as little as possible is overlooked and forgotten;
the different parts of the work are seen in relation to each other.

Remember that the play was written to be performed. Watch how it guides and controls what should happen in performance.

The conventions of the Edwardian theatre are implied in Shaw's dialogue: for instance, the characters show no recognition of the fact that they are on a stage in the presence of an audience.

Style of dialogue, in lengthy rhetorical speeches, witty exchanges, or vigorous Cockney slang, is some indication of appropriate style of performance, while at the same time contributing significantly to the shaping of the character of the speakers.

Do not neglect stage images which convey meaning, for instance: the setting for the last scene, in which the cannon is used as a seat.

Remember which characters are present on stage apart from those speaking. Consider the effect of Undershaft's silent presence for part of Act II and Barbara's in Act III.

Consider the emotional effect of Barbara standing alone near the end of Act II, while the band plays and most of the others march out past her. Note how the intermittent beating of the drum contributes to the excitement of particular moments in Act II.

Organising your study

Firstly, be sure that you can recall the general outline of the play's development. Test yourself with the following simple questions:

What characters appear in each Act, and in what order do they appear?
What different settings are used in the play and which scenes are they used for?
What happens in each of the three Acts?

Consider how Act I prepares for the subsequent development of the play, especially:

what information it gives about Lady Britomart's family and about the Undershaft tradition;

what impression it gives of Lady Britomart's attitude to her children;

how the contrast between Barbara's beliefs and activities and her father's is set out.

Plot and structure

Both terms refer to the author's arrangement of his material. The summaries in Part 1 of these notes concentrate on the plot, or order of incidents in the story. The structure gives meaning and value to the story and contributes to the artistic effect of the play.

The subplot

The story of Bill Walker intersects with the story of Barbara, Cusins and Undershaft in the play's structure. Parallels, variations and contrasts between the two stories draw attention to particular themes. Examples are:

Bill's sovereign is connected in our minds with Undershaft's cheque;

the blow Bill deals to Jenny Hill is a demonstration of the physical force which Cusins and Undershaft discuss.

Consider what Bill and Undershaft hope to gain for their money. Can you find another instance in the play where getting value for money is in question? Which characters are most interested in money? Are all the characters interested in money for the same reason?

Do you think the play is more interesting and enjoyable because it represents physical force in the character and story of the bully, not just in Undershaft's dynamite?

The dynamic structure

List major and minor examples of opposition and conflict. Here are some to start you off:

(*a*) Undershaft and Cusins express systematically opposed views of the Salvation Army in Act II;

(*b*) Bill strikes Jenny Hill;

(*c*) Stephen defies his mother in the first scene of Act III.

Dramatic success depends to a considerable extent on how the discussions are relieved and enlivened by interruptions or simultaneous happenings. Shaw had particular difficulty with the last Act.

What, if anything, is gained by the division of Act III into two scenes, in different locations?

What incidents, major or minor, enliven the final scene? (Even essential stage moves, entrances and exits are worth noting)

Now look at Act II and examine the skill with which Shaw uses incidents to illustrate or emphasise points raised in the discussion.

The character plot

The selection of characters and placing of them in relation to each other is another structural element.

Distinguish the major characters from the minor ones. Undershaft is obviously a major character: the central conflict of the play would disappear without him. Sarah and Peter Shirley are obviously minor characters. How important is Lady Britomart?

There are two young women among the characters, in addition to Barbara. In what ways do they contrast with Barbara?

Think of the range of wisdom and foolishness represented among the characters. Where on this spectrum would you place the following: Barbara, Cusins, Undershaft, Lady Britomart, Charles Lomax, Stephen, Peter Shirley, Bill Walker, Mrs Baines?

Another obvious grouping would be on class lines. Do you perceive direct contrasts or parallels between particular characters on different sides of the class barrier? (It is worth noting where the class grouping overlaps with the grouping according to age and experience.)

Why should Stephen, and not Barbara, have been brought into the first scene with Lady Britomart? Consider Stephen and Barbara as brother and sister and in relation to the inheritance.

Theme

Any story or subject is given meaning and relevance to other people's experience in the world by the way the author presents it. Discovering such meanings, or themes, involves becoming aware of general reflections arising out of the specific story and characters. A number of themes are likely to emerge from any considerable work. Here are some of the themes with which *Major Barbara* is concerned:

(*a*) idealism and realism;
(*b*) wealth and poverty;

(c) conversion;
(d) growth and change in morality and religion;
(e) inequality and equality;
(f) the nature and source of power;
(g) force, or violence;
(h) warfare and the fighting spirit;
(i) the value and effectiveness of Christian behaviour.

Do you want to add any others? Some of these themes are closely related to each other. Does it seem to you that any one theme includes most of the others? See how many of the themes listed you can illustrate with at least one reference to a particular aspect of the play, or passage in the play. Here is an example of how an essay on one theme may be based on a series of relevant observations:

INEQUALITY AND EQUALITY
(a) this is shown visually in the contrast between Lady Britomart's house and the Salvation Army shelter;
(b) when Barbara introduces Peter Shirley to her father, the great inequality of their income is emphasised;
(c) Shaw directs that Bill should instinctively touch his cap (a mark of respect) when Undershaft offers to give ninety-nine pounds, but when Barbara has been left desolate he offers to shake hands with her (a mark of equality);
(d) the play contains many references to what people are worth, ranging from the sovereign with which Bill tries to buy the freedom of his soul, to the sum Cusins agrees to accept on entering the firm;
(e) Bill realises that he is unequal to Todger Fairmile as a wrestler;
(f) Undershaft refers to the social system in Perivale St Andrews as a hierarchy in which everyone looks down on the man below him;
(g) Barbara speaks of all men and women as children of one Father and has herself tried to live on thirty shillings a a week;
(h) towards the end of the play, she addresses God as an equal.

Characterisation

Consider what means Shaw has used to make us imagine particular characters as we do. The example of Andrew Undershaft will serve here:

What does Lady Britomart say about her husband in the first scene?
How does Undershaft behave in Lady Britomart's house?
Do you get a different impression of him from his behaviour at the shelter?
List the various nicknames that Cusins applies to him and consider what each implies.
What does Undershaft say about his early life?

Are you persuaded that he is always right in his debates with Cusins and Barbara?
Can you find evidence that Undershaft is not altogether trustworthy?

How far is the character acceptable as a portrait of an early twentieth-century man, and how far is it a personification of an abstract idea or general force (for example, capitalism or authority)?

The style of the play

Examine the play as a comedy

Find two or three examples of verbal jokes, or amusing speeches.
Look for examples of Shaw's expression of a serious point in humorous form.
Are there elements in the situation and the way it develops that strike you as amusing, or more fantastic than realistic?
What is it in (a) Charles Lomax and (b) Lady Britomart that makes you laugh? Is Stephen a comic character?
Look for two or three points in the play where Cusins's sense of humour is evident.
Consider the ending of the play. Contrast its mood with the mood of the end of Act II. Do you find it a straightforward happy ending?

Symbolism

Look in the dialogue for evidence of the symbolic value (abstract or metaphysical associations giving a special significance to material quantities or objects) of *fire* and *dynamite* in the play.
Undershaft follows Barbara's reference to the shelter, 'At the sign of the cross', with 'Perivale St Andrews. At the sign of the sword', opposing a traditional emblem of battle and authority to the Christian emblem of salvation through suffering. What ideas and emotions do you associate with the drum in Act II?
Can you identify a symbolic action, or incident, in Act II?
To what extent is Perivale St Andrews presented as a symbol of the perfect society (or Utopia)?

Style in the dialogue

Collect some examples of Shaw's use of short, pithy statements, or aphorisms, such as 'Genuine unselfishness is capable of anything', and think carefully whether they can be interpreted in more ways than one.
Look closely at one of Undershaft's longer speeches, for example that

beginning 'Have you every been in love with Poverty, like St Francis?' in Act II. Note how it is constructed, looking out for such features as: the rhetorical repetition of sentence patterns; the use of questions and answers, or commands, within the speech; the piling of phrase upon phrase, or parallel sentence upon sentence, to a point of climax; twists away from one pattern to another; variations of rhythm.

Look through one scene, noting how and where Shaw varies this kind of rhetorical speech with a more natural, conversational style. The second scene of Act I, or parts of Act II, may be examined for Shaw's skill in bringing in different speakers to give variety to the dialogue.

Do you think there is enough variety of style in the dialogue of the last scene of the play?

Do you think any part of the play gets monotonous because Shaw presents a single point-of-view at too great length?

The Preface and the play

When you know the play well, go back to the Preface and consider whether it is more concerned with (a) the play or (b) independent discussion of social and political problems.
    What have you gathered from the Preface about:
        'Crosstianity'
        Shaw's view of legal punishments
        His attitude to social and political violence?

Find three examples in the Preface which illustrate Shaw's argument that morality is relative to circumstances.

How effectively does the play support Shaw's statement in the Preface that 'Money is the most important thing in the world'? Does the play show any other force that might be considered equally important?

Answering questions on the play

These processes are involved: (*a*) developing your ideas; (*b*) planning the order of presentation; and (*c*) drawing evidence from the text to support your argument. Do not quote at length unless you want to examine an entire passage closely; a line or even a phrase will usually serve.

Here is an example of how a question may be tackled.

QUESTION: *What is the function of Stephen in the play?*

The answer might follow these lines:

(*a*)   Under the usual law of inheritance, he would succeed to his father's position and fortune. Setting him aside signifies a revolutionary break of social continuity.

90 · Hints for study

(b) Stephen's timidity and conventionality contrast with Barbara's courage and freedom of spirit. This destroys conventional notions of male and female character.
(c) Stephen is a conventional moralist, with no doubts about right and wrong. Thus he is the embodiment of the attitude Undershaft – and, through Undershaft, Shaw – is attacking in the play.
(d) Shaw makes the character a vehicle for his criticism of contemporary Liberalism.
(e) Stephen, as well as Barbara and Cusins, undergoes an education in the course of the play: his mother first opens his eyes to aspects of reality and starts the process which leads to his little rebellion against her; seeing Perivale St Andrews completes the process.
(f) This additional thread increases the interest of the plot, especially in Act III where the sense of things happening is most needed to counterbalance the long speeches of the debate.
(g) Stephen is a sort of fool, contrasting with the cheerful fool, Charles Lomax. By making us laugh at some of his characters, Shaw promotes the mood of optimism needed to counterbalance the grim truths he has to reveal about human nature and society.

A possible conclusion would point out how Shaw uses the character to strengthen the argument of his play and, at the same time, to solve technical problems and to achieve desirable artistic effects.

Now select the material you would use to answer this question:

Discuss Shaw's view of women and their place in society, as revealed in Major Barbara.

Part 5

Suggestions for further reading

The text

The texts of *Major Barbara* used in the preparation of these Notes were:

(a) *The Bodley Head Bernard Shaw: Collected Plays with their Prefaces*, edited by Dan H. Laurence, Max Reinhardt/The Bodley Head, London, 1971, volume 3, pages 9–200.
(b) the edition first published by Penguin Books, Harmondsworth, 1960, and reprinted many times since: this text is also available in an edition published by Longman, London, 1964.
(c) the screen version first published by Penguin Books, Harmondsworth, 1945/6, approved by Shaw, and reprinted as late as 1957.

Students will probably wish to use one of the two paperback editions. If possible, they should also consult in a library the Bodley Head edition for additional material not included in the paperback editions. (See also p. 15.)

Other works by Shaw

(a) Plays particularly interesting to compare with *Major Barbara* are:

Mrs Warren's Profession, in Bernard Shaw, *Plays Unpleasant*, Penguin Books, Harmondsworth, 1946, and frequently reprinted; also in *The Bodley Head Bernard Shaw*, volume 1.
Heartbreak House, Penguin Books, Harmondsworth, 1964, and frequently reprinted; also in *The Bodley Head Bernard Shaw*, volume 5, and in the Longman edition.
Saint Joan, Penguin Books, Harmondsworth, 1946, frequently reprinted; also in *The Bodley Head Bernard Shaw*, volume 6. Compare Joan with Barbara.

(b) Letters:

Bernard Shaw, *Collected Letters*, volume 2, edited by Dan H. Laurence, Max Reinhardt, London, 1972, contains a number of letters relevant to *Major Barbara*, the most important being that written to Gilbert Murray on 7 October 1905 and given on pp. 565–6.

Works by other authors for comparison with *Major Barbara*

BARKER, HARLEY GRANVILLE: *The Voysey Inheritance*, 1905 (published by Sidgwick & Jackson, 1910). A contemporary treatment of a similar theme, written for the same theatrical repertory as *Major Barbara*.

BRECHT, BERTOLT: *Saint Joan of the Stockyards* (*Die heilige Johanna der Schlachthöfe*, 1929–30). English version in Brecht, *Plays*, volume 2, Methuen, London, 1962. Set in Chicago, but based on *Major Barbara*, freely adapted to lead to different moral judgments about capitalist society.

DICKENS, CHARLES: *Oliver Twist* (1838). Shaw's main literary model for the low-life characters of Act II. Available in Penguin edition, Harmondsworth, 1966.

WILDE, OSCAR: *The Importance of Being Earnest* (1899). Lady Britomart begs comparison with Wilde's Lady Bracknell; it is instructive to compare the comic methods the two playwrights use in presenting English upper-class society. Available in *The Portable Oscar Wilde*, Penguin Books, Harmondsworth, 1977.

Life of Shaw

There is no very satisfactory life of Shaw at present. The most detailed attempts are:

HENDERSON, ARCHIBALD: *Bernard Shaw: Playboy and Prophet*, Appleton and Company, New York and London, 1932.

HENDERSON, ARCHIBALD: *Bernard Shaw: Man of the Century*, Appleton and Company, New York, 1956.

General studies containing interesting commentaries on *Major Barbara*

BENTLEY, ERIC: *Bernard Shaw*, New Directions, Norfolk, Connecticut, 1947; second edition, Methuen, London, 1967. Discussion of Shaw's thought, not a play-by-play investigation. Still a standard work.

BERST, CHARLES A.: *Bernard Shaw and the Art of Drama*, University of Illinois Press, Urbana, 1974. Includes discussion of Undershaft in the light of Machiavelli and William Blake.

COMPTON, LOUIS: *Shaw the Dramatist*, University of Nebraska Press, Lincoln, Nebraska; Allen and Unwin, London, 1971.

DUKORE, BERNARD F.: *Bernard Shaw, Director*, University of Washington Press, Seattle; Allen and Unwin, London, 1971. On Shaw as a producer of his own plays.

DUKORE, BERNARD F.: *Bernard Shaw, Playwright*, University of Washington, Seattle; Allen and Unwin, London, 1973. Discusses the various versions of the play.

DUKORE, BERNARD F.: Introduction to Bernard Shaw, *Major Barbara: A Facsimile of the Holograph Manuscript,* Garland Publishing Inc., New York and London, 1981, pp. XII-XXII. Discusses the stages of Shaw's work on the play.

FERGUSSON, FRANCIS: *The Idea of a Theater*, Princeton University Press, New Jersey, 1949. Stimulating, with critical reservations about the play.

GIBBS, A. M.: *Shaw* (Writers and Critics series), Oliver and Boyd, Edinburgh and London, 1969. Probably the best short book on Shaw.

KAYE, J. B.: *Shaw and the Nineteenth-Century Tradition*, University of Oklahoma Press, Norman, 1958. Reads *Major Barbara* in the light of Carlyle and Dickens.

MCCARTHY, DESMOND: *Shaw,* Macgibbon and Kee, London, 1951. Highly intelligent contemporary criticism.

MEISEL, MARTIN: *Shaw and the Nineteenth-Century Theater*, Princeton University Press, New Jersey; Oxford University Press, London, 1963. Crammed with information and interesting observations. Useful on the influence of music on Shaw's dramatic writing, as well as on his indebtedness to Victorian melodrama.

MILLS, J. A.: *Language and Laughter: Comic Diction in the Plays of Bernard Shaw*, University of Arizona Press, Tuscon, Arizona, 1969. A linguistic approach.

MORGAN, MARGERY M.: *The Shavian Playground: An Exploration of the Art of George Bernard Shaw*, Methuen, London; Barnes and Noble, New York, 1972; Methuen University Paperback, 1974. By the author of these notes.

VALENCY, MAURICE: *The Cart and the Trumpet*, Oxford University Press, New York, 1973.

WEAT, ALICK: *A Good Man Fallen Among Fabians*, Lawrence and Wishart, London, 1950. A Marxist interpretation, seeing *Major Barbara* as Shaw's farewell to socialism.

WISENTHAL, J. M.: *Marriage of Contraries: Bernard Shaw's Middle Plays*, Harvard University Press, 1974.

Some important essays

MEISEL, MARTIN: 'Shaw and Revolution: the Politics of the Plays', in Norman Rosenblood (ed.), *Shaw: Seven Critical Essays*, University of Toronto Press, Toronto and Buffalo, 1971, pp. 106-33. Highly recommended; informed and thoughtful.

WATSON, BARBARA B.: 'Sainthood for Millionaires', *Modern Drama*, volume 11, 1968, pp. 227-44. Lively argument.

The author of these notes

Margery Morgan graduated at Bedford College, University of London, and became a lecturer in medieval literature and modern drama at Royal Holloway College, University of London. She then was a Senior Lecturer and subsequently Reader in English at Monash University Melbourne, Australia. She is now Reader in English at the University of Lancaster. Her publications include *A Drama of Political Man: A Study in the the Plays of Harley Granville Barker* (1961) and *The Shavian Playground: an Exploration of the Art of G. B. Shaw* (1972). She has edited Shaw's *You Never Can Tell* (1967) and Granville Barker's *The Madras House* (1977). She has also written articles on medieval literature and drama, on Shaw, Granville Barker, Strindberg, Australian theatre, and recent English dramatists, and is the author of *Pygmalion* in the York Notes series.